Professional Development for Teachers

Teaching and Assessing Skills in
English as a
Second Language

Peter Lucantoni

CAMBRIDGE
UNIVERSITY PRESS

CAMBRIDGE UNIVERSITY PRESS
Cambridge, New York, Melbourne, Madrid, Cape Town, Singapore, São Paulo, Delhi

Cambridge University Press
The Edinburgh Building, Cambridge CB2 8RU, UK

Published in the United States of America by Cambridge University Press, New York

www.cambridge.org
Information on this title: www.cambridge.org/9780521753562

First published 2002
Reprinted 2006, 2008

A catalogue record for this publication is available from the British Library

ISBN 978-0-521-75356-2 paperback

Transferred to digital printing 2009

Contents

This book is dedicated to my friend and colleague, Costas Djapouras.

Foreword

Teaching is a complex and demanding profession. All over the world, societies change in response to new knowledge gained, technological developments, globalisation and a requirement for an ever-more sophisticated and educated population. Teachers are in the forefront of such social change, responding with speed and confidence to the new demands made of them, in terms of both their knowledge and the way in which they teach. This series is intended to help them in their adaptation to change and in their professional development as teachers.

Curriculum changes worldwide are putting increased emphasis on the acquisition of skills as well as subject knowledge, so that students will have the ability to respond flexibly to the swiftly changing modern environment. As a result, teachers must be able both to teach and assess skills and to adjust their own teaching methods to embrace a wider range of techniques for both teaching and assessing in the classroom. The books in this series are practical handbooks which explore these techniques and offer advice on how to use them to enhance the teacher's own practice.

The handbooks are written by teachers with direct experience of teaching and assessing skills at this level. We have asked them to write for their readers in such a way that the readers feel directly supported in their professional development. Thus, as well as tasks for students, there are tasks for teachers, pauses for reflection and questions to be answered. We hope that readers will find that this mixture of the practical and the professional helps them, both in their practice and in their own sense of what it means to be an effective teacher in this modern, changing world of international education.

Dr Kate Pretty
Series Editor

Acknowledgements

As always, a big thank you to Lydia, Sara and Emily for allowing me the time to write books. Thanks also to my students, student teachers and colleagues, past and present. Special thanks to everyone at Forum Language Centre, Nicosia, Cyprus, and in particular: Maria Christou, Stavroulla Marangou, Katerina Viacoumis, Dora Shiakallis and Vincent Allan, as well as Viota Kontoloucas at the English Learning Centre in Limassol, Cyprus – their patience and support have been extremely valuable. Many thanks to everyone at Cambridge International Examinations and Cambridge University Press who helped me to make this book a reality: Paul Beedle, Camilla Erskine and Una Yeung.

1 Introduction

Purpose and contents

It is hoped that this book will prove useful to teachers throughout the world who are involved in teaching English as a Second Language (ESL) at IGCSE and similar levels, and who need up-to-date input on some of the current issues in teaching and assessing language skills. While many teachers will be preparing students for examinations, this book does not focus purely on examination skills, but will hopefully provide teachers with a broad overview of ways in which they can assist students in the classroom through language skills development, as well as focusing on grammar and vocabulary.

When giving examples, I have endeavoured wherever possible to draw on my own classroom experiences as a teacher and teacher trainer, but at the same time I have not attempted to be dogmatic about the teaching of English. I am a firm believer that there is no best way to teach – what is effective and suitable for one teacher in one situation may frequently be ineffective and unsuitable for another teacher in a different teaching situation. However, there are common areas of quality teaching practice which we all need to strive for, and which are discussed in various parts of this book.

In many ways I am in a somewhat privileged teaching position because I only have to deal with relatively small groups of students, who are, for the most part, fairly motivated to learn. I appreciate that there are other teachers who daily have to deal with large groups, and others still who may be dealing with students who lack any real motivation. Some teachers will be preparing students for external examinations, while others may not; some will teach their students for as few as two or three hours each week, while in some cases they may have as many as ten or more contact hours. The variations in teaching and learning situations are endless, and thus a book of this type cannot realistically advocate one particular approach.

However, what this book does attempt to do is to provide teachers with an understanding of the importance of the role of skills in teaching English. Increasingly nowadays we see curriculum and syllabus development making steps towards a skills-focused design. In teacher training, initial courses as well as INSET and diploma courses are highlighting more and more the importance of language skills and task-based learning.

In Chapter 2, the role of language skills in ESL is discussed, with emphasis on sub-skills and their importance for the student. Furthermore, the reasons why teachers need not teach grammar and vocabulary explicitly are considered. Chapter 3 looks at some key issues in teaching and learning ESL: communicative language teaching, student interaction in the classroom, a task-based approach to teaching and learning, and the structural approach to language teaching. Chapter 4 focuses on the ESL curriculum, in particular on how teachers can make their curricula more student-centred. There is also a section on lesson planning in this chapter. Chapter 5 discusses the language skills in ESL, while Chapter 6 is concerned with the teaching and development of these skills, dealing with both receptive and productive language skills in detail. In Chapter 7, how language skills (particularly writing) are assessed is discussed in detail.

What is ESL? Is it different from EFL?

'English as a Second Language' is the term used to refer to the role of English in those countries where people generally use their native language (L1) at home and with their friends and family, but may use English (L2) at school or work. Additionally, ESL is the term given to the role of English in countries where it is used widely, for example in business and government, but where it is not the first language of the indigenous population. In Britain, ESL is distinguished from EFL (English as a foreign language), the latter being used for the role of English in countries where it is taught as a school subject, but is not used as the language of instruction in education nor in business and government. In the USA, the term EFL is not normally used, with ESL serving for all the above situations.

Teacher activity 1.1

Describe your local teaching situation. Which term, EFL or ESL, would you use to describe it? Why? What do you regard as the key differences between the two?

The importance of English in a global context

Whether we choose to use ESL or EFL, there is no doubt that English is a world language, with more than 60 countries where 'English is now the dominant or official language' (Crystal 1999: 106). The importance of English throughout the world in education, business, government and social situations continues to grow, despite the understandable desire of people to preserve their own 'native' languages. The growth in the number of people using English as either a first or second language continues to provide the language with a wealth of varieties, dialects and accents, none of which can be said to be 'the standard'. As David Crystal points out, 'a totally uniform, regionally neutral, and unarguably prestigious variety [of English] does not yet exist worldwide' (ibid.: 111). Each and every country which uses English has its own particular identity and culture, and while to some extent it can be said that British English, American English and Australian English tend to dominate, 'we are a long way from uniformity' (ibid.: 111).

Students who are preparing for examinations in English at a fairly high level of language proficiency (for example, IGCSE) need to have had exposure to a wide range of material, including personal, factual and advertising texts, as well as other genres. These texts should be selected not only for their content, but also for their international perspective, and should strive to be 'culturally fair though it is recognised that they cannot be, nor is it intended that they should be, culturally free' (UCLES 1997: 1). Teachers need to imitate the stand taken by examination boards when choosing texts for teaching purposes, and ensure a rich spectrum of global input. The syllabus for the UCLES IGCSE ESL 2003 examination states that the rationale for 'English as a Second Language is based on the widespread use of English as the medium of instruction and as the language of commerce or the environment. The subject matter of the examination material will reflect this international perspective' (CIE 2001: 1). It is important to point out, however, that students may sometimes face texts (whether written or spoken) which they feel uncomfortable with because of a lack of familiarity with the subject matter.

2 The role of skills in ESL

This chapter considers the four language skills of reading, listening, writing and speaking, and the ways in which they interrelate. Finally, it looks at the focus of teaching on integrated language skills, rather than grammar and vocabulary, whilst incorporating the latter where necessary.

Learning to use language skills

People who have a skill demonstrate the ability to do something well. We talk, for example, about football skills, a skilful pianist, a skilled carpenter and doing something skilfully. Thus, when we talk about skill in a language, we are referring to the ability to use that language well. Of course, how well or badly we do something is a very subjective area, and this is just as true when we refer to language. But what exactly are language skills?

Language skills are usually grouped as:
- **receptive skills** – listening and reading;
- **productive skills** – writing and speaking.

People who use a language have a number of **sub-skills** within each of the four main skills. In other words, the main skills can be further divided into a number of types of skills. Thus, within the skill of writing, we can identify a number of sub-skills – writing a letter to a friend is a very different skill from writing a letter of resignation to an employer, for example. Similarly, writing a report about the problem of noise pollution in London is a different writing skill again. Listening to a university lecture is not the same as listening to an announcement at the airport. Speaking to a friend is different from speaking to a judge in a court of law. Therefore we need to employ different sub-skills for each task: listening for details, reading for a general understanding, writing notes, answering questions in an interview situation, and so on.

What other sub-skills can you think of for the four main language skills (i.e. reading, listening, writing and speaking)? The diagram below may help you to organise your ideas.

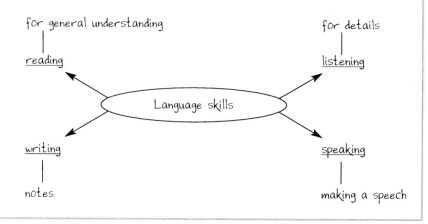

Every language user's proficiency in the various language skills will be different; furthermore, every language user's needs in each of the skills will differ from the next language user's. One of our roles as teachers of ESL therefore is to help students to develop those particular skills which (a) they are weak in; and (b) they need for a particular purpose. Furthermore, it is our role to help our students to select the sub-skill which is appropriate for the task in hand. We need to encourage student independence so that students do not always rely on their teachers to tell them which particular sub-skill to employ. As an example, if you look at any upper-intermediate to advanced level examination which assesses reading and writing skills, you will discover that a variety of sub-skills are required in order to answer the various questions.

Using an examination paper with which you are reasonably familiar, or a text with questions from a coursebook, analyse the questions and decide which language sub-skills are required by students in order to answer the questions.

Students need the ability firstly to decide which skill is required for a particular language task, and then to implement that skill. In a real-life situation, someone who wants to find the name 'Cambridge' in a telephone directory will not start at the letter 'A' and read every entry until they arrive at 'Cambridge'. Someone who has command of the various reading sub-skills would obviously skip all the 'A' and 'B' entries, and look at the entries under 'Ca'. If someone wants to find the TV listings in their daily newspaper, they go immediately to the TV page, skipping sport, fashion and business. Once they have found the TV listings, skim reading changes to scanning – to find what is on at nine o'clock, or to check when the news is on.

We do not read everything in order to find one single piece of information. While this may seem obvious, think about what many students might do if asked to find a particular piece of information in a text or magazine or book. How many would think that they needed to read the whole text in order to find the information? Unless students have been trained to **skim** read and **scan** read, and to understand that in order to find one or two details it is not necessary to read everything, they will surely continue to read slowly, worrying constantly about words that they do not comprehend. The same applies to the other language skills, where students must be able to select the most appropriate sub-skill for the task in hand.

It is worth mentioning here the importance of **register**, i.e. the variations in a person's spoken or written language. Register, or style, will change depending on the context, the audience, the topic and so on. Thus students need to be aware of the need for a particular register in a given situation. For example, a letter of complaint written to a bus company will require a different register from that used in a note written to a friend, despite the fact that both employ writing skills. The former will need to be formal, with addresses and salutations; the latter may be written in note form, and could be single words rather than complete sentences and paragraphs. Similarly, the register used to speak to a person of some importance will be completely different from that used in conversation with a friend. Students therefore need to identify the correct register for a particular situation or task, and then select the appropriate skills and sub-skills in the implementation of that register.

The problem teachers face is trying to help students to overcome their fear of unknown words and to understand that it is not necessary to understand everything in order to get the general idea of something, or to find a specific detail. Students may appreciate that reading everything is not the best approach, but training them to implement a more efficient method is not always easy. So, how can teachers do this?

The key is to help students to build up their confidence so that when they come across an unknown word or phrase, they will have the courage to skip it and carry on, or to consider meaning by use of contextual clues. The alternative is to labour over 'difficult' words and not make any progress. Students' confidence in reading will improve through exposure to texts accompanied by relevant tasks; and, of course, the same is true of the other skills. Furthermore, we want students to appreciate that first language users employ the same sub-skills in real life, as shown in the telephone directory and other examples earlier. Only through employing these same language skills will second language students ever become accomplished language users.

Teacher activity 2.3

Look again at some of the texts and questions which you examined in Teacher activity 2.2. What do you think would be the best strategies for your students to use in answering the questions?

After briefly looking at the text to see what it is about, it is important for students to identify the key elements in the questions. The first step we would want them to take is to find and underline the **key word(s)** in each question. This has two results: firstly, it helps students to become more familiar with the text and its content and, secondly, finding the key words helps students find the required details in the text, *without having to read and understand every word*. The next step is to look at the text, skimming through it in order to find the key words already identified in the questions. Of course, words from the text may have been paraphrased in the questions, for example 'uninhabited' may appear as 'nobody lives there'. However, the strategy explained above is an effective one. Finding key words in the text will help students to find the required information.

One further important part of this approach is that students must be encouraged to work within a time limit. Without this, students may simply slip back into the habit of reading everything and worrying about not understanding every word in the text. Teachers therefore need to set a time limit for activities which require skimming and scanning reading skills.

While the above advice is clearly based on examinations and comprehension-type questions, the same is also true in other learning situations. If, as teachers, we provide students with 'authentic' tasks, then we should do everything we can to ensure that they employ 'authentic' skills.

In activities which require students to listen to a text, sub-skills should be employed before students actually listen. For example, students could be asked to predict what they are going to hear, to guess the outcome of a discussion, or to look at pictures related to the text. During the listening itself, it is important for students to ignore language which is irrelevant to the task in hand, and to focus on particular speakers, or on certain pieces of information. See Chapter 5 for more information on teaching and developing skills in ESL.

What are integrated language skills?

While it is probably true to say that in real-life situations (and by that I mean situations outside the classroom) language skills are sometimes employed independently of each other, this is not always the case in the teacher–student environment. In real life, we may listen to a radio broadcast or watch a TV show without doing very much else (from a language skills point of view). However, when do we give students the opportunity to listen to something without there being a task attached to it? Isn't it the case that we ask students to listen to something and take notes? Or answer the comprehension questions which follow? Or discuss what one person said to the other? Do we ask students to read something purely for the fun of it, as we do in the real world? Don't we usually tell them to read and then write a summary? Or answer the multiple-choice questions? There are, of course, teachers who do provide their students with the opportunities to use language in real-life situations using real-life skills, but I suspect that they are few in number. Having said this, many teachers may feel that they are not in a position to provide these real-life experiences in the classroom, either because of a lack of confidence, or because of some external control by the school, or the examination at the end of the year.

However, the point here is that language skills are rarely used in isolation, and therefore skills should not be learned and developed in isolation. Language skills are **integrated**; they 'cooperate' with each other. Obviously, it is not possible to hold a conversation with someone unless two language skills are employed: speaking and listening. Even writing a letter involves reading and rereading what has been written. In the classroom, this principle of integrating language skills is vital.

In many reading and writing examinations, certain questions specifically require students to focus on texts (reading) and extract details which then need to be presented in a written form (writing). Thus two skills are being integrated. In listening papers, students often need to listen and take notes or answer questions. In the classroom, we may ask students to prepare for a final writing task through reading texts, interviewing people, and even listening to recorded information. All of these examples show that language skills cannot stand in isolation, and even though we may need to focus on one particular skill, this will invariably lead to the use of other skills.

Look at the newspaper article below. Using this text, what activities can you think of to help your students integrate their language skills?

The trouble with mosquitoes

All over the world, the Earth's skies are buzzing with a bloodthirsty enemy credited with defeating modern armies, and killing millions of people each year. Only about the size and weight of a grape seed, this dangerous enemy is descended from insects that probably emerged during the Jurassic period and survived the dinosaurs on which they fed. Indeed, the 2,500 or so species of mosquito that plague us are so supremely adaptable that they have so far resisted all our attempts to control them and the deadly diseases they carry. But now scientists are preparing to fight back in order to wipe out one of the most common mosquito-borne diseases: malaria.

Malaria is transmitted by female mosquitoes which carry a parasite called plasmodium. The parasite infects humans from the insect's saliva when it drinks its victim's blood. The World Health Organisation estimates that there are 500 million cases of malaria each year, with plasmodium becoming more and more resistant to insecticides.

However, in laboratories around the world there is increasing confidence that scientists will acquire the ability to spread a genetic gene throughout the populations of dangerous mosquitoes, making it impossible for them to pass malaria on to humans. Until now, spreading genes throughout a species was something only evolution was capable of over millions of years of natural selection. But scientists think it might be possible to transform the malaria-carrying mosquito into a subtly different species – still a bloodsucking nuisance, but no longer a killer – within two to twenty-five years of releasing the first genetically modified (GM) insects. A team of scientists has already inserted a gene into mosquitoes that makes it impossible for the parasite that causes malaria to gain a foothold. Last year, a transgenic mosquito was created, one whose offspring would also carry the inserted gene.

Based on 'Scientists to fight malaria with GM mosquitoes', by James Meek, *Guardian Weekly*, p. 3, 6–12 September 2001, and 'The trouble with mosquitoes', by Lisa Sabbage, *Sunday Mail* (Cyprus), p. 24, 16 September 2001.

As the text is obviously meant to be read, the focus for integrating other skills needs to be on writing and speaking, and possibly listening as well. Students could be encouraged to investigate the topic further, perhaps through accessing an encyclopedia or a CD-ROM, and presenting more facts about mosquitoes. The text would easily lead into project work, perhaps focusing on the problem of mosquitoes in the students' own country.

Why not teach grammar and vocabulary?

When students have reached the level of IGCSE or similar, it is likely that they will have been exposed to a very wide range of language, in terms of both grammar and vocabulary. While without doubt there will be areas of language which are weaker than others, the focus of learning at this level needs to be on language skills development. Students are not going to be assessed on discrete language items through cloze exercises, nor asked to deal with sentence transformations and word-building exercises. Assessment is not based on percentages and grades, but on performance. Students need to be able to demonstrate that they are confident in using the language to communicate effectively, and this is usually achieved through tasks designed to encourage 'whole language' use.

Thus we return to the topic of integrating language skills in the classroom, and encouraging students to lose their fear of unknown words (both read and heard). We need to build their independence in using language in 'real' situations. While the accurate use of a wide range of language is important at this level, far more important is the ability to use language to complete tasks and to communicate effectively. Thus whether writing a book review or preparing an oral presentation, both provide practice in how to use language in different, real-life situations. Vocabulary and grammar are still present, of course, and assist in performing the tasks; however, vocabulary and grammar are not learned explicitly – they are not the result of the task. Students begin to understand that perfection in language is not necessary in order to communicate effectively. However, an integrated approach to language teaching and learning will of course find room for focusing on specific areas of language where necessary.

Teacher activity 2.5

Using the newspaper article from Teacher activity 2.4, which
(if any) areas of grammar or vocabulary could students focus on?
Which areas do you think your students may have difficulties with?

This text, while short, does contain some vocabulary which may cause students to worry if they are not used to employing the skimming and scanning skills mentioned above. You may therefore decide that the text could be used to focus on challenging but useful vocabulary (e.g. 'supremely', 'adaptable', 'wipe out', 'laboratories', 'infects', 'resistant'), or a specific grammar area (e.g. prepositional phrases, such as 'credited with', 'descended from', 'spreading throughout', 'inserted into', 'transmitted by', 'resistant to').

Teacher activity 2.6

Choose a text from a newspaper or magazine which you would like to use with your students. Consider how you could (a) use the text to help your students to integrate their language skills; and (b) exploit specific language areas (e.g. grammar and vocabulary) within the text.

LOOKING BACK

- ◆ How might your understanding of language skills and sub-skills affect your classroom teaching?
- ◆ Can you foresee any problems in encouraging students to use specific strategies when dealing with tasks?
- ◆ How feasible do you now think it is to adopt an integrated skills approach to your teaching?
- ◆ What do you think would be an ideal balance between skills and grammar and vocabulary in your situation?

3 Key issues in teaching and learning

This chapter discusses key issues relating to the teaching of ESL, in particular:

- the role of communicative language teaching;
- how to organise your class to enable effective learning;
- the use of a task-based approach.

Communicative language teaching

In Chapter 2, I made the point that at IGCSE and similar levels, the focus of learning needs to be on language skills development. Students have to be able to demonstrate that they can use language to communicate effectively in a variety of situations, using a range of skills and sub-skills. The teacher's role is therefore to encourage communicative language use in the classroom.

Much of what goes on in the ESL classroom today is labelled 'communicative'; in other words, the approach used by the teacher emphasises the importance of 'communicative competence' (Hymes 1972). Many teachers claim to follow a communicative approach, but fail to fully understand what is involved. This section will attempt to clarify what the term means.

Teacher activity 3.1

Consider what you do in the classroom. Write down five words or phrases which describe your approach to teaching.

Communicative language teaching (CLT) is a move away from more grammar-based and single-skills approaches, which has come to prominence in the last 25 to 30 years. Prior to the move towards communicative language teaching, the profession toyed with various methods and approaches: grammar-translation, audio-lingualism, cognitivism, situational language teaching, and so on. For more detailed reading on approaches and methods, there are many texts available. However, four highly accessible texts are:

- Richards and Rodgers, *Approaches and methods in language teaching;*
- Nunan, *Language teaching methodology – a handbook for teachers;*
- McDonough and Shaw, *Materials and methods in ELT – a teacher's guide;*
- Harmer, *The practice of English language teaching.*

Language which helps students to understand and to express themselves in various situations is pivotal in communicative language teaching. Thus, functions and their language exponents, such as describing ('It looks like a ...'), warning ('Be careful!'), requesting ('Can I have a ...?') and refusing ('No, I can't ...'), and knowing when to use them, are essential. Furthermore, the ability to use language to perform various tasks, such as problem-solving, as well as using it to interact with people, are emphasised in this approach. Language exponents which the student needs are the focus. Grammar in the traditional sense of the word is not taught explicitly.

This approach is important in teaching and learning ESL at IGCSE and similar levels because it '(a) makes communicative competence the goal of language teaching; and (b) develops procedures for the teaching of the four language skills that acknowledge the interdependence of language and communication' (Richards and Rodgers 2000: 66). The UCLES IGCSE ESL syllabus for 2003 (CIE 2001: 1) states that the aims of the syllabus are to enable students to:

> develop the ability to use English effectively for the purposes of practical communication in a variety of second language situations and in foreign language situations where applicable; form a sound base for the skills required for further study or employment using English as the medium; develop an awareness of the nature of language and language-learning skills along with skills of a more general application.

Any other approach in preparing students for this examination would, no doubt, struggle to achieve the aims which UCLES CIE sets out in this document. On the other hand, no doubt there are teaching and learning situations in which a more 'academic' approach achieves the 'sound base for the skills' identified in the syllabus.

Which of the following statements do you think apply to you and your teaching situation? Try to give reasons.

1 Meaning is more important than structure.
2 Structure-based dialogues are used.
3 Mastery of the language is the goal.
4 Language is used in contexts.
5 Pronunciation need only be understandable.
6 Drilling is the central technique.
7 Communication should start at a very early stage in learning.
8 All language skills are given equal prominence.
9 Use of L1 is forbidden.
10 Communicative (rather than linguistic) competence is the aim.
11 Language becomes more complex with progress.
12 Teachers assist students in any way that motivates them.
13 Errors often contribute to language creation.
14 Fluency is more important than accuracy.
15 Language use is controlled by the teacher.

List adapted from Finocchiaro and Brumfit 1983.

As Richards and Rodgers (2000: 66) point out, 'communicative language teaching is best considered an approach rather than a method'. Teachers are free to interpret the 'rules', and thus a wide variety of classroom techniques is feasible.

Hopefully, the move away from teaching which produced students who were 'structurally competent' but often 'communicatively incompetent' (Johnson 1981) has provided teachers with an approach which will encourage and motivate students to transfer their structural knowledge into real-life situations. It is fundamentally important, however, to remember that 'it is clearly not possible to engage in purposeful communication in a language without being able to formulate the structures of that language as well' (McDonough and Shaw 2000: 25). Consequently, it is essential for teachers to interpret the rules and strike a balance between consolidating structures and developing communicative competence in their ESL students. This means providing students with real-life situations in which they are able to use the language they have learned, while at the same time providing them with help and support with structures and vocabulary, if needed.

How does this affect us, the ESL teachers?

Normally, there are no questions specifically on grammar in IGCSE ESL and similar examinations: students are not usually required to 'transform' sentences, put verbs into the correct tense, nor change sentences from active to passive voice. Furthermore, there are rarely any questions which require students to change nouns into adjectives or verbs. What the examinations try to do is to provide students with a variety of tasks which assume knowledge of structures and the ability to form comprehensible utterances. Assessment is normally based on task completion, rather than on the tools used to perform the task, although in some tasks this may not be the case. Teachers therefore need to ensure that learning at this level is focused on tasks and problem-solving. Of course, if students have problems with certain language areas, then it is the teacher's job to provide assistance: this is what I would perceive as being quality teaching practice.

Groups, pairs or individuals?

Teacher activity 3.3

For this activity, refer to a coursebook you are currently using, or one which you have used in the past and with which you are familiar. How many activities in the book require students to work alone? In pairs? In groups? What language or skills are practised through these activities? Reflect upon your own class management in this area, based on texts you have used.

For real communication to take place, students need to be interacting with someone else, whether this is you as the teacher, with other students in the classroom, or with an 'unseen' audience, such as when writing a letter to someone. How 'real' this communication is will depend very much on the type of activities which the students are asked to perform. Nowadays, examinations attempt to be communicative by providing students with reasons for carrying out examination questions. For example, questions for assessing extended writing skills often provide a *reason* for writing, as well as an *audience*. Texts for reading are often *authentic*, taken from, or closely based on, sources which students themselves might come across.

It follows that, in order for students to be prepared effectively for examination questions, they need to have had practice with communicative tasks in the classroom. Thus it is essential that we provide them with opportunities for pairwork and groupwork. However, it is equally important to avoid situations in which 'get into pairs' or 'in your groups' become more or less automatic instructions for the setting up of each and every classroom activity. Teachers should not regard students working on their own as bad classroom practice! Individual study gives students the chance to 'relax from outside pressure' (Harmer 2000: 248), helps to develop reading skills, and means that they 'can rely on themselves rather than other people' (ibid.: 248). In fact, in my experience, teachers may shy away from classroom pairwork and groupwork because they see inherent problems.

Teacher activity 3.4

Make a list of what you consider to be the advantages and disadvantages of using pairwork and groupwork in your classroom. Use a table like the one below to organise your ideas.

Groupwork		Pairwork	
Advantages	**Disadvantages**	**Advantages**	**Disadvantages**
	Students may use L1 (especially in monolingual groups)	Fairly easy to set up	

Obviously what is needed, as in so much of the teaching profession, is to strike a balance so that both the students' needs and the teacher's objectives are met.

A task-based approach

We have discussed at some length what communicative language teaching is, and the importance of providing students with opportunities for communicative language practice in the classroom. I shall look at curriculum planning and development in detail in Chapter 4, but here it is worthwhile considering what a task-based approach actually is.

Some of you may be aware of how in the past foreign languages were taught in schools, using rather traditional translation methods, with little or no 'real' language being produced. The focus was on structure and memorising lists of words; probably the language of instruction was the L1, rather than French or Spanish or whatever the L2 happened to be.

Many students may have completed two or three or even more years of studying a foreign language but were unable to communicate in it. Exposure to chunks of language at the word and sentence level, without exposure to authentic language as used by native speakers, nor with opportunities to produce the language naturally, were much to blame for this inability to communicate.

It is nowadays commonly accepted that there are three conditions which are essential for effective language learning in the classroom, and which 'apply to all students, regardless of their individual cognitive styles' (Willis 1999: 11). There is also a fourth condition, which is seen as desirable.

Teacher activity 3.5

What do you think Willis means by 'individual cognitive styles'?

Teacher activity 3.6

Based on your teaching experience, what do you regard as essential and desirable conditions for language learning?

The four conditions are:
- **exposure** to the target language, at a comprehensible level, both written and spoken;
- **use** of the target language to perform various meaningful tasks;
- **motivation** to communicate in the target language through reading it and listening to it, and speaking and writing it;
- **instruction** in the target language, with opportunities to focus on form and vocabulary.

Teacher activity 3.7

What are your views on the conditions above?

However, even if the essential and desirable conditions exist in the classroom, it is likely that much of the language interaction will be teacher-centred and teacher-generated, and therefore somewhat different from 'real-world interaction' (ibid.: 11). Teachers may need to change their approach in order to provide students with more opportunities to use the target language through topic selection, initiating and responding, and turn-taking. Many communicative language examinations in spoken English assess candidates on their 'interactive communication' or 'fluency': 'The candidate can respond to change in direction of the conversation and perhaps initiate new topics [and] play a part in a discussion' (CIE 2001: 7); candidates for the UCLES Certificate in Advanced English (CAE) speaking examination 'are expected to listen carefully ... show their ability to organise their thoughts and ideas ... [and] should pay attention while their partner is speaking. [Furthermore,] candidates are expected to negotiate and collaborate with each other ... and report on the outcome of their discussion' (UCLES 1999: 50).

Examinations in written English also attempt to provide candidates with tasks which focus on real-life situations, as discussed earlier in this chapter. The IGCSE ESL examination requires candidates to 'identify, organise and present given material in a particular form [and to] demonstrate the ability to describe, report, give personal information' (CIE 2001: 7).

The implications for ESL classroom teaching and learning at the levels being discussed here are thus very clear. By providing students with tasks in which a focus on language is not immediately important, teachers can provide opportunities for natural interaction. Students learn to use the language they have already acquired in order to complete certain tasks; only then does the teacher need to focus on structure and vocabulary, if there are weak areas in language use. This may not of course be practical in large teaching groups, but it would certainly be desirable. *Exposure* to and *use* of the target language through the setting of student-centred tasks maximises 'opportunities for students to put their limited language to genuine use, and to create a more effective learning environment' (Willis 1999: 19). This in turn provides the *motivation* for students to communicate. The desirable condition, *instruction* in the target language, is provided by the teacher as a result of their monitoring of the tasks performed by the students.

Teacher activity 3.8

Consider your current teaching style. How does it compare with the task-based approach to teaching and learning described above?

The task-based approach therefore means the teacher using techniques which provide students with opportunities to work in pairs or groups, using language which they have already acquired in order to solve tasks. Furthermore, students must be given the chance to work independently of teachers, and not to rely on them for selecting topics or initiating interaction. Through this environment, language should be stimulated, but above all, developed.

LOOKING BACK

- ◆ What is your understanding of a task-based approach to teaching?
- ◆ How feasible is it in your situation to ensure that the four conditions for language learning (see p. 17) are actually met?
- ◆ What problems do you think students may face in learning through a task-based approach?
- ◆ Do your students take external examinations? If so, how useful do you consider the ideas discussed in this chapter might be in helping them to prepare effectively?

4 The ESL curriculum

'Curriculum' here is used in its broad sense, i.e. it covers all decisions about syllabus, aims and objectives, methodology, assessment and evaluation, etc. In this context, this chapter discusses curriculum planning and development, focusing on a student-centred approach, and then considers lesson planning in more detail.

Curriculum planning and development – a student-centred approach

Teaching students of ESL who have a high proficiency in the language is never an easy task because the abilities and various proficiencies within such a group are bound to be disparate. Whereas beginners and elementary students tend to be more homogenous in terms of their abilities, those students at a higher level are less so. They come to class with varying degrees of competence, and the teacher's role can therefore be complex and demanding when having to deal with the various needs of a group of advanced students. As students become more proficient in a language, they will of course acquire and develop a wide range of language and skills to a greater or lesser degree. One of the teacher's roles is to help students to 'automatise' all the language they know, so that less time is spent on thinking about small chunks of language and more time on interpretation and negotiation, and communicating interactively.

In order to deal realistically with these demands, it is vital for teachers to consider the needs of students, and then to select and even produce materials to meet those needs. There should be negotiation with students in order to establish not only their needs, but also to ascertain their individual learning styles, their interests, their goals and so on. Of course, there may be many teachers who are not in a position to influence to any degree the choice of teaching materials, nor the way in which the materials are delivered in the classroom; furthermore, there may not be the opportunity to effectively assess students' needs. However, the preference is for teachers to be in a position to take a more student-centred approach, and have the time and resources to consider the needs and learning styles of students.

Consider one of your advanced level ESL classes. What are the needs of the students? Are the needs of individual students different from those of the class as a whole?

In considering students and their course of instruction, there are certain steps which need to be followed (adapted from Hedge 2000: 342). Note that these steps should be considered as cyclical, and not linear.

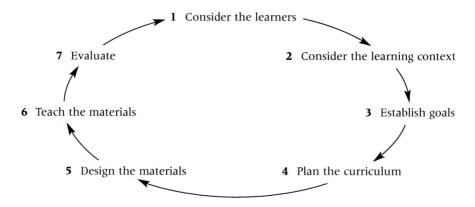

1 Consider the learners

7 Evaluate

2 Consider the learning context

6 Teach the materials

3 Establish goals

5 Design the materials

4 Plan the curriculum

In the first steps, issues such as age, gender and interests need to be considered. If a topic-based curriculum is planned, establishing where students' interests and goals lie is vital, as authors do make various suppositions. Furthermore, it is important to consider how students will communicate with each other, and of course the size of the class (i.e. the number of students) will have an important part to play. Equally important are issues such as class time and on which day(s) of the week the class meets. As a teacher of ESL, you may or may not be in the position of designing your own curriculum, or assisting in the design of one; whatever the case, however, you are probably able to produce some of your own teaching materials. This therefore means that having a broad understanding of students' needs is desirable.

Probably the best way to determine students' goals and interests, their perceived strengths and weaknesses, and their learning styles, is through a simple questionnaire. Once the data has been collected, suitable goals can be considered (step 3). Goals are broad (e.g. to achieve effective communication in English); whereas outcomes and even aims are specific (e.g. to be able to write a letter in reply to a job advertisement), and may be based on general preparation for an examination such as IGCSE ESL, as well as focusing on particular areas of language and skills development. Obviously, if a course is designed to prepare students for a specific examination, whether it be IGCSE or any other external assessment, then the main goal must be to do simply that; however, within the curriculum, other goals need to be specified. These will be based on the data collected from students, as well as on the teacher's own continuous appraisal of the students in the classroom. As mentioned earlier in this chapter, advanced level students will tend not to be homogenous in terms of proficiency, and therefore it may be the case that a teacher will need to address a wide variety of needs in the curriculum planning stage (step 4).

Step 4, planning the curriculum, must be based on the goals identified in the previous step, and should take into consideration as far as possible the needs and goals of individual students as well as those common to the whole group. It is likely that a coursebook will be used, but this may need to be supplemented if it does not provide all the necessary support for students. Remember that the teacher's job is to teach the *students*, not the *coursebook*.

It is advisable at the start of a course to spend some time looking through the coursebook, checking the 'menu' (i.e. contents), in order to identify areas in which you feel that supplementary materials, or even a change of approach, may be necessary. Of course, a cursory glance at a coursebook is never enough to really know whether or not the materials are going to be suitable for your particular students – a coursebook cannot be written with such a small audience in mind. The only way to know for sure is to actually use some of the materials before selecting the coursebook. This will then give you some idea of how suitable (or unsuitable) the materials are.

Teacher activity 4.2

Look at the 'menu' of the coursebook you are currently using, or which you intend to use. To what extent does it meet the needs of your students, as identified in Teacher activity 4.1?

Step 5, designing the materials, is the result of the planning stage. This is where you may need to develop or adapt the coursebook in order to make it 'fit' the students; alternatively, you may find that the coursebook is satisfactory and meets most of the needs of the group, but that you require additional materials. Whatever the case, unless you are in a position whereby you are able to design a complete course, use the coursebook as a foundation and build materials around it. Apart from anything else, you need to be flexible, so that when needs arise *during* a course of study (step 6), you are able to respond and provide the necessary materials to deal with the particular need. Remember that we are trying to provide a student-centred approach, the fundamental rule of which is to respond to what students actually need, and not provide a curriculum which ignores them.

On the other hand, using a coursebook can limit a teacher's freedom to use alternative resources, such as the Internet, supplementary materials and materials produced by the students themselves. If we agree that in a student-centred approach it is essential to respond positively to students' needs, then it follows that we need to use whatever resources are available in order to do so. If this means abandoning the coursebook for a period of time, then so be it. There is now a wealth of material available through the Internet, some of which will be immediately accessible, whereas other material may need to be adapted. Newspapers and magazines continue to provide a readily available source of texts in the form of articles, advertisements, and so on. Something I have done over the years is to collect texts from sources which I think may at some stage be of use in the classroom; these texts include not only newspaper articles, but also leaflets written for tourists, information leaflets, advertising brochures, and so on. The BBC offers free subscription for teachers and students to various publications which contain an enormous amount of useable material. One further source is the type of magazine written specifically for students. While these are not free, publishers (such as Mary Glasgow Magazines) are usually more than willing to provide free samples. (See Appendix B for contact details.)

Finally, step 7, evaluating, does not simply refer to some sort of assessment of students. It covers the much broader principle of the teacher's self-evaluation, and evaluation of the teaching materials used during the course: 'evaluation means assembling evidence on and making judgements about the curriculum including the processes of planning, designing, and implementing it' (Skilbeck 1984: 238 in Hedge 2000: 351). As teachers, we must never assume that what we do is always the most effective approach or technique; it is vital to reflect and self-analyse, with a view to making changes. The point here is not to find fault, but to find areas which can be improved on and developed. Although evaluation is given as the final step, it is something which should be happening throughout the whole process. Evaluation needs to be planned in the same way as all other aspects of teaching need to be: in advance.

Lesson planning

The practicalities of actual classroom teaching give rise to a host of questions:
- How do I make sure that I cover everything in the syllabus?
- How do I manage the class effectively?
- What should I do if things don't go well?
- How can I judge if my lesson was successful?

A lesson plan should help you in finding the answers to many of these questions.

The layout and design of a lesson plan varies from teacher to teacher, but it is generally assumed that certain elements of information should be included. Usually, a lesson plan will consist of a 'top sheet', and a 'continuation sheet'.

Top sheet

A top sheet should cover:
- aims;
- assumed knowledge;
- anticipated problems;
- materials, aids and equipment;
- personal development.

Teacher activity 4.3

What do you consider to be your planning strengths and weaknesses? For example, do you find it difficult to identify your lesson aims?

Aims

Aims are what you as a teacher need to aspire to in order to provide your students with the tools (whether the skills or the language, or both) to be able to do something by the end of the lesson that they could not do at the start – a **student outcome**. As such, aims are key to planning – without aims, it is impossible to plan an effective lesson. Make sure aims are both student- and linguistically-based, and are verifiable. For example, 'students will use reported speech' is not a satisfactory aim because it does not identify in what way the language point will be used – is it being introduced or revised? Will students need to produce it or will they only use it receptively? Will it be heard or read? Spoken or written? and so on. Furthermore, it is not verifiable. Much better might be: 'students will practise using reported speech for describing past events (e.g. road traffic accident) in a role-play situation'. Here it has been specified exactly what the students will be doing with the language item, and it is verifiable through the role-play activity.

Furthermore, take care not to confuse student outcomes with activities. 'To do a role play' is not an aim – it is a student outcome. You need to specify what the aim of the role-play activity is, for example: 'to consolidate vocabulary related to previous work in class'.

Assumed knowledge

Consider what knowledge students will already have before the lesson in question ('assumed knowledge'). Do they need to know anything before they can deal with what you plan to do? Thinking back to the role-play example above, what exactly do students need to know before they can participate in the role play? Have the language and vocabulary items already been introduced? If not, how can the role play go ahead?

Anticipated problems

What linguistic problems do you think students may have with the lesson? If it is a language lesson (i.e. one which deals with vocabulary, structure, phonology, functional language), will students face problems with the form? The meaning? The sounds? If so, how can these problems be overcome? What solutions can you find to the problems? If you are using a communicative approach, how important do you think it is to anticipate problems with language?

Materials, aids and equipment

It is important to consider this, even though it may seem trivial. Teachers are busy people, and it is easy to forget key items.

Personal development

This may be a somewhat contentious item to include in a lesson plan 'top sheet', but I feel it is vital for any teacher who is concerned about their own professional development. A 'personal development' section is often included in lesson plans produced by teachers on certificate- and diploma-level training courses. The content is usually based on a trainer's feedback to a teacher made during lesson observation, and thus the 'personal development' items are, more often than not, someone else's point of view. In the 'real world' of teaching, teachers may not be observed, and thus the impetus for personal professional development has to come from teachers themselves. Reflection is not easy, and it is certainly time-consuming, but looking back and trying to identify areas for improvement is a commendable act. If a teacher can make a habit of reflecting on lessons taught, even if there seem to be no areas of weakness, the simple act of thinking about what you did is extremely valuable. It is also step 7 in the cycle discussed earlier in this chapter.

Continuation sheet

After the top sheet comes the continuation sheet, in other words, the lesson procedure, a step-by-step account of what is going to take place during the scheduled lesson time. The format depends very much on individuals, and who is going to read it. If the lesson in question is going to be observed, it may well be that a certain 'in-house' format is a requirement. Whatever the case, the continuation sheet should ideally make the lesson more or less 'reconstructable', i.e. able to be used (or at least understood) by others.

Teacher activity 4.5

Describe in detail a recent lesson you have taught. Do this in the form of a plan which includes both a top sheet and a continuation sheet. Make sure your continuation sheet gives room somewhere for the following: stage, aims, timing, interaction, aids and resources, procedure.

Which layout you choose to use is entirely up to you. Your plan may look something like this:

Stage	Aims	Time[1]	I/A[2]	Aids	You	Them
4	Highlighting written form on WB with phon	5/20	T-SS	WB	Ask SS for written form, write on WB, include phon should (not) + have + V3 ☐ They shouldn't ☐ ↘ have gone. /ðeɪ ʃʊdəntəv ɡɒn/	SS give form + phon: *They shouldn't have gone.*

[1] Use both absolute and cumulative time, so that you do not have to keep adding up the minutes to find the total
[2] interaction pattern
T = teacher, WB = whiteboard, SS = students

Alternatively, it could look similar to this:

Stage	Procedure	Aim
Warmer 5 mins S–S	SS move around room, look at each other's. clothes. T tells SS to stand in pairs back to back, describe what partner is wearing.	Get SS talking and revise clothes vocab

It is important that you analyse language items so that you yourself are clear about meaning, form and phonology. For example, think about concept questions and what response you anticipate students will make; highlight the form clearly so that you have it ready for writing on the board if necessary:

> They shouldn't have gone.
> should (not) + have + V3

Make sure you are aware of the sounds, stress and intonation of the target language, and write it on your plan:

> ☐　　　　☐↘
> They shouldn't have gone.
> /ðeɪ ʃʊdəntəv gɒn/

Once completed, your lesson plan should be a flexible guide, and should not be regarded as something set in stone. Remember once again that we need to respond to our students' needs, and the teacher who blindly follows a plan cannot possibly react to situations as they arise in the classroom: 'Flexibility is the characteristic we would expect from the genuinely adaptable teacher' (Harmer 2000: 258).

A lesson plan should, ideally, be a reusable document; in other words, once used, it might be filed and referred to for a future lesson or lessons. However, the post-lesson reflective process is essential in order to identify those areas of the lesson (and of course the plan itself) which were perhaps weaker than others. The question to ask oneself is 'Would I teach that lesson in the same way on a different occasion?' If the answer is 'no', we need to identify how it could be taught differently next time. Changes may not be major – they could be small adjustments in, for example, the timing of an activity, or a change in the interaction pattern at a certain stage of the lesson. These types of minor change would not normally require any significant amendments to a lesson plan, while more major weaknesses might only be solved through the complete abandonment of a plan. As teachers, the most important element here is to go through the process of post-lesson self-reflection.

Teacher activity 4.6

Think back to a recent lesson you have taught. Identify three strengths and three weaknesses in the lesson. How would you teach the lesson differently next time?

 LOOKING BACK

- How much of a problem is mixed-ability teaching in your situation?
- How possible is it for you to evaluate and change your teaching programme?
- What is not normally included in your programme which you think should in fact be there?
- Does a task-based approach to teaching and learning make lesson planning easier or more difficult for you?

5 The language skills

As discussed in Chapter 2, there are two categories of skills:
- the receptive skills – listening and reading;
- the productive skills – speaking and writing.

These skills are now considered in more detail, with emphasis on how to teach them effectively, and in particular how to motivate students to learn.

The receptive skills – listening and reading

Teaching methodology textbooks vary in the order in which the teaching of the language skills are dealt with. I have chosen to deal with the receptive skills first because listening and reading provide the input of language into the student's 'store', which is later used to produce language through speaking or writing. Without input, there can be no output. Furthermore, there are certain principles and teaching methods which are common to the receptive skills. Lastly, listening and reading skills usually develop before the productive skills of speaking and writing in L1 acquisition.

Teacher activity 5.1

What do you think the common features of listening and reading might be?

Certainly, both listening and reading involve some sort of coherent and cohesive text, as well as a 'receiver', someone who 'receives' the text. There must also be an interaction between the text and the receiver, in other words, the receiver needs to *listen* or *read*. Finally, the receiver must be able to understand and interpret the input of language, whether listened to or read. Listening or reading without being able to interpret the language would not result in comprehension and communication.

In our daily lives, we read and listen to a great variety of texts, from a range of sources. Linguists nowadays agree that this input of language (i.e. what we read and listen to) can be divided into two very broad categories: items which are *interesting*, and those which are *useful*. Of course, the categorisation may well be different for everyone, and there may be some overlap between the categories.

Teacher activity 5.2

Add examples to the following table. There are some already done for you (but of course you may not agree with these!)

Read		Listen to	
Useful	Interesting	Useful	Interesting
Instructions for building a cupboard	Novel	Weather forecast	Pop concert

When we listen or read, we do so for a particular **purpose**: we read the instructions for building a cupboard, because without doing so we would probably find it difficult to construct the cupboard; we listen to a pop concert because we like that style of music. Furthermore, we usually have an **expectation** of what we are going to listen to or read in that we turn on the radio at 6 p.m. because we know that the pop concert is due to start; we open the instruction booklet for the cupboard because we know that inside we will find out how to construct the cupboard; if we look at the front cover of a novel, or indeed the 'blurb' on the back cover, we will have expectations about the content of the book. Thus we rarely, if ever, read or listen to something without wanting to, and we nearly always have an aim in doing so.

This of course applies to the real world: but what happens in the language classroom? In other words, how does the theory inform classroom practice? How often do we allow our students a choice? When do we give them a real purpose? Do our students ever have expectations about something they are going to listen to or read? Are they given the opportunity to think about something before the cassette is turned on or the book is opened? The principles of purpose and expectation need to be reflected in the classroom in the tasks which teachers ask students to perform. In doing so, we can improve realism and motivation, and encourage more effective communication.

In order to assist students in the development of their receptive skills, it is important to focus on the sub-skills or specialist skills which we employ when listening or reading. (See Chapter 2 for more on sub-skills.) The use of these sub-skills will to some extent determine success in comprehension and interpretation of a text (whether listened to or read). Efficient readers, for example, will 'switch' between sub-skills, depending on the type of text they are reading. Even when dealing with one particular text, an efficient reader will switch modes, depending on what information they want or need to extract from a text. Readers know when to use skimming skills to obtain a general idea about a text, and when to scan for more specific details, and are therefore **active** rather than **passive**. Efficient readers interact with a text.

Teacher activity 5.3

Look at these examples of pre-listening and pre-reading exercises from a coursebook for IGCSE ESL. How do the exercises encourage the reader to 'interact' with the text?

Pre-listening

Exercises 1–6 from Lucantoni, Cox and Glover (2001: 27–8)

1 How many different methods of transport can you and your partner think of? Make a list.

2 There are nine different methods of transport hidden in the wordbox. How many can you find? Are they the same as the ones you thought of in Exercise 1? The words are written horizontally, vertically and diagonally.

B	M	N	E	V	C	A	E
U	I	E	H	G	A	W	K
S	O	C	O	A	B	C	I
R	T	P	Y	H	A	A	B
C	D	Z	C	C	L	M	R
S	F	A	G	J	L	P	O
V	O	S	T	A	O	E	T
C	F	E	R	R	O	R	O
I	Q	D	A	K	N	L	M
Y	T	C	I	R	N	C	G
P	L	A	N	E	V	X	S

3 Which method of transport do you think is the best for going on holiday? Why? Does it depend on the type of holiday? Discuss with your partner.

4 Make a list of the advantages and disadvantages for each method. An example has been done for you.

Method	Advantages	Disadvantages
Car	stop when & where you like	traffic jams

5 In Exercise 3, did you consider the cost of each method? With your partner, rank the methods from 1–9, with 1 being the most expensive and 9 the cheapest. What factors do you need to think about when deciding on the cost of each method?

6 Look at the list a–c below. Discuss with your partner which of the methods of transport you listed in Exercise 4 would be best for each of these holidays.
  a beach holiday
  b sightseeing holiday in one town
  c skiing holiday

Pre-reading

Exercises 1–6 from Lucantoni, Cox and Glover (2001: 127–8)

1 What do the following symbols and letters mean in 'Internet language'? Discuss with your partner, and add to the list any more that you know.

:-)	:-(	STR8	BFN	RU	2DAY
IC	LOL	L8R	JK	TTYL	

2 Why do you think people use these codes? What is the benefit of writing 'IC' instead of 'I see 'or 'I understand '?

3 What effect do you think that using language codes might have on written language in the future? Do you think it might cause people to write less? Why/Why not? Is it possible that language codes could appear in formal written language? Can you think of any codes which you already use in your writing?

4 You are going to read a newspaper article with the title: 'E-mail sends coded warning to English teachers.' Discuss with your partner what you think the article might be about. Write down two points which you think might be made in the text.

5 Read these definitions of nine words which have been removed from the text you are going to read. Match each definition with a word from the list following. Work on your own and do not use your dictionary yet.

   a the words and phrases used in a language
   b the short forms of words
   c something not done carefully or neatly
   d a possibility that something bad will happen
   e to represent, or to be a sign of something
   f developed
   g short, clear, with no unnecessary words
   h messages or letters
   i technical words and expressions

abbreviations	jargon	signify
concise	lexicon	sloppy
evolved	missives	threat

6 Compare your answers with your partner's. Do you agree? Use your dictionary for help.

Teachers need to provide students with a purpose for reading or listening, through texts which will stimulate and motivate. Teaching activity 5.3 has identified some ways in which this can be done. Ron White (1981, excerpt in McDonough and Shaw 2000: 113) suggests various stages for a reading lesson:

Stage 1 – arouse the students' interest and motivation by linking the topic of the text to their own experience or existing knowledge. Give some pre-reading/focusing questions to help them do this.

Stage 2 – give them points to search for in the text, or ask the students to suggest points.

Stage 3 – after reading, encourage a discussion of answers.

Stage 4 – develop into writing by using the information gained for another purpose.

The texts which teachers have to use with their students are, more often than not, outside their control, either because they are using a coursebook, or because texts are prescribed by the school. However, even if there is no opportunity to select texts, every teacher should consider how best to create a purpose for reading in order to stimulate and motivate students to interact with a particular text.

It is more or less standard practice nowadays to provide students with pre-, while- and post-tasks for listening and reading texts (see the coursebook examples in Teacher activity 5.3), and many current materials follow this approach. The pre-tasks phase should encourage students to 'tune in' to the text and to think about or predict the content, thus preparing themselves for purposeful listening or reading later on.

Teacher activity 5.4

Look at some of the listening and reading units in a coursebook you are currently using. What type of tasks are set as pre-listening or reading tasks'? Is there variety between the units? Make a list of possible pre-tasks (for example, using pictures to assist in content prediction, or a quiz).

You will probably have identified a variety of pre-tasks, such as focusing on pictures which relate to the text, or activities which require students to brainstorm a particular topic or vocabulary area. Prediction tasks, such as guessing the content of a text, or deciding what will not be in a text, are also valuable activities for students to perform before listening to or reading the text itself.

Tasks which take place as students actually listen or read ('while-tasks') are designed not only to make students active, but also to encourage them to interact with the text. Examples of while-tasks could be: following the order of ideas within a text; note-taking; predicting the next part of the text; completing a chart – the list is endless.

Post-listening and reading tasks should in some way make use of what has been read or listened to, through, for example, a discussion of the content, or as a motivator for research. Other activities are wide ranging, and include role play, projects and listening to or reading other texts which may contrast with the original. There may be areas of language within the text which could form the focus for follow-up work, for example, the use of modals, or a particular set of vocabulary.

Teacher activity 5.5

Look through a coursebook you currently use. Select a unit which you have recently taught and consider what additional types of pre-, while- and post-activities you could give to your students.

Although I have so far discussed listening and reading without any differentiation, it must be mentioned here that despite the many similarities between the two skills, there are also differences. Firstly, a listening text is not 'static' in the way that a text for reading is, which can be read and reread as and when the reader wishes. A text which is spoken is momentary, unless of course it is on a cassette or video which can be rewound and replayed. When a written text is read, it is the reader who determines the speed of the activity – this is not the case with a spoken text. Certainly, in a conversation, it is common for people to ask each other to repeat something, but this is not possible if you are watching a film, or listening to the radio. Thus students need to acquire the necessary skills for dealing with 'momentary' language, something which we shall consider later on in this book.

Spoken language is different from the written word in other respects. When we write, more often than not, we strive for accuracy – we 'check' for spelling mistakes, missing punctuation, and so on. We may write an initial draft, then change things around, and produce a final draft, attempting to produce something which is logical, coherent and correct. Thus, in general, a text which is read by an ESL student will be more or less error free, because of the processes described above. Not so with spoken language, which is frequently filled with moments of hesitation, repetition, and reformulation, all of which goes on in writing, but is not apparent, whereas in spoken language it is often not amended. Students have to know what to ignore in spoken language and to focus on the main message and ideas: 'They do this in their own language ... we must make sure they can do the same in English, although clearly in acceptable stages' (Harmer 2000: 212).

The productive skills – speaking and writing

While we have seen that there is in fact common ground between the receptive skills of listening and reading, there are possibly fewer similarities between the productive skills. However, consider the following:

- Speakers and writers want to communicate a message.
- Both have in mind a receiver (i.e. the listener or reader).
- There is a purpose in speaking or writing the message.
- A process of selection of language takes place, bearing in mind the receiver and the purpose of the message, as well as the context in which the communication is taking place.
- The message can only be communicated in a form which the receiver can make sense of.

Clearly, therefore, there are similarities. However, when we consider the differences, it is interesting to note that the list is longer.

Use the table below to compile a list of the differences between spoken and written language. Some of the table has been completed for you. Can you think of any other areas which are not listed? How might what you do in your classroom be affected by the identification of these differences?

	Spoken	Written
Age	extremely ancient	comparatively recent
Importance		
Distribution	universal among humans	
Acquisition		by puberty, if at all
Dominated by	mothers	
Modification		
Paralinguistic features		punctuation
Frequency of use		
Durability	transient	
Feedback availability		
Formality level	speech often more informal	
...		

McDonough and Shaw (2000: 151) point out:

> As a language skill, speaking is sometimes undervalued or, in some cases, taken for granted. There is a popular impression that writing, particularly literature, is meant to be read and as such is prestigious, whereas speaking is often thought of as 'colloquial', which helps to account for its lower priority in some teaching contexts.

However, speaking is not simply saying something which is written: speaking involves the use of a complex range of language and sub-skills, such as knowing when to initiate conversation, turn-taking and knowing when to stay quiet!

As with the receptive skills, it is vital for students to be motivated to use and be interested in using the language in either the spoken or written form. A lesson to develop speaking skills which begins with the words 'Now we're going to have a debate about capital punishment' is more likely to produce blank faces and total silence than an interesting and useful discussion; the teacher who asks students to write about 'The advantages and disadvantages of military service' should not be surprised if the result is less than satisfactory. If we want our students to speak and write we need to do the following:

- Provide students with topics which are relevant and interesting to them, something which can only be done if teachers actually investigate, i.e. perform some sort of needs analysis. We need to find out what our students' interests are, and what topics they would like to know more about. Learning language can and should be integrated with learning about the world and developing our students' knowledge of global issues.

- Ensure students have some previous knowledge or experience of the topic. This can be done through pre-reading tasks, such as viewing a video, or listening to people discussing the topic. Rarely, if ever, should we expect our students to engage with a text which focuses on a topic or vocabulary area with which they have no knowledge or experience.

- Give students some sort of motivation for speaking or writing. As discussed earlier, we rarely if ever speak or write for no purpose, so by giving our students a reason for doing a language task, we hope to increase their motivation. If the task is realistic, and if it can result in realistic feedback to the student, motivation will be further increased.

- Provide students with time to prepare. Far too often teachers do not give students time to formulate and prepare their ideas, whereas preparation time is an essential element in the process of developing the productive skills.

Teacher activity 5.7

Look through an examination paper with which you are reasonably familiar. Consider in what ways you could develop the material in order to fit your own teaching situation. For example, what activities could you ask your students to do in order to ensure that texts are not received 'cold'?

LOOKING BACK

◆ To what extent do you think your students benefit from knowing about purpose and audience in their writing?
◆ How important are the various language skills in your particular teaching situation?
◆ How can students be encouraged to appreciate the importance of speaking as a language skill, especially if it is not formally assessed?
◆ As a result of reading this chapter, are there any changes to your current teaching practice that you would consider making?

6 Teaching and developing the skills

Let us now deal with each of the skills on a more individual basis and consider the ways in which we can teach these skills and help students to develop their proficiency in using them.

Listening

What do good listeners do in order to interpret messages? 'They segment the stream of speech into its constituent sounds, link these together to form words, chain the words together to form clauses and sentences and so on' (Nunan 1991: 17). This 'bottom-up' approach is not, however, always adequate in that it does not allow the listener to take account of context. Meaning does not lie solely within the words themselves (whether spoken or written) but also within the head of the receiver. Utilising this extra knowledge, i.e. the knowledge which is not in the message itself, in order to make an interpretation, is referred to as the 'top-down' approach.

The amount of extra knowledge required will be determined by the difficulty of the listening text for the listener. Brown and Yule (1983: 00) suggest the following as key factors affecting the difficulty of tasks based on listening skills:

- the number of speakers;
- the speed of the speech;
- the accents of the speakers;
- the role of the listener (participant or eavesdropper);
- the response required;
- the interest of the listener in the topic;
- the grammar, vocabulary and assumed knowledge of the topic;
- the support given to the listener in the form of diagrams, pictures, etc.

We have identified that listeners need to use both the knowledge received and their own knowledge of the world in order to interpret messages, thus using both bottom-up and top-down approaches. First, listeners **process sounds,** using sub-skills, which includes recognising:

- word boundaries (where one word ends and another word starts);
- contracted forms;
- lexical items;
- stress, intonation, pitch and rhythm.

Then, they **process meaning**, which involves:

- organising the sounds into meaningful 'chunks';
- discarding or ignoring irrelevant language;
- anticipating what is coming next.

These three listening sub-skills are key in the IGCSE ESL listening paper and other, similar examinations.

McDonough and Shaw (2000: 135) summarise the processing of sounds and meaning:

> **Processing skills are often discussed under two related headings, which are tabulated below (the equivalencies are not exact, but they capture the points made in this section):**

Processing sound	Processing meaning
Phonological	Semantic
Lower-order/automatic skills	Higher-order skills of organising and interpreting
Recognition of sounds, words	Comprehension
Localised: the immediate text	Global: the meaning of the whole
Decoding what was said	Re-construction after processing meaning
Perception	Cognition

Finally, after processing sounds and meaning, listeners use their knowledge of the context of the text and their knowledge of the world in order to fine tune their interpretation of the message.

Teacher activity 6.1

Bearing in mind the above, what are the implications for the ESL teacher and student with regard to various classroom listening tasks? Consider different types of listening tasks (such as listening for gist, listening for detail and listening to take notes).

When we listen in our first language, this processing takes place automatically. However, this is not the case with L2. Furthermore, we should remember that many of the listening tasks which our students are confronted with have been designed to 'test' them in some way (see Brown and Yule's key factors above). Our students, initially, need a reason for listening: to engage in some sort of social interaction, to find out information, for entertainment, to follow a lecture or lesson, to confirm expectations and so on. For you as a teacher, having a reason or purpose for an activity helps to identify 'the various dimensions which need to be taken into account when designing listening materials' (Hedge 2000: 243).

We are not concerned in this book in using listening as a means to focus on specific language areas (e.g. grammar or vocabulary). As outlined in previous chapters, the purpose here is to *assist students in the development of their language skills in order to perform various tasks*. A standard procedure with this in mind might be as follows (compare with White's stages for a reading lesson mentioned in Chapter 5):

- Teacher prepares for the listening task(s) and makes sure that students have understood what they have to do, using pre-listening task(s).
- Students perform the task(s), using while-listening task(s).
- Teacher provides an opportunity for feedback and discussion, followed by extension activities, using post-listening task(s).

Pre-listening tasks may include some or all of the following (this list is by no means exhaustive):

- content prediction through reading the title, headings, key vocabulary items and so on;
- commenting on a visual;
- reading something based on the topic;
- looking at comprehension questions in advance;
- discussing the topic.

It is important that the pre-listening stage 'contextualises the text, providing any information needed to help students appreciate the setting and the role relationships between participants' (Hedge 2000: 249).

Teacher activity 6.2

Using a coursebook with which you are familiar, consider whether the pre-listening tasks achieve the aim set out above.

While-listening tasks should in some way link back to tasks completed in the pre-listening stage, and may focus on **extensive** or **intensive listening**. Extensive listening develops overall understanding of a text, listening for gist if you prefer. Students may be asked to correctly sequence a series of pictures, follow directions on a map or diagram, tick items heard (e.g. vocabulary), complete a chart or table, or check predictions made during pre-listening. You will notice that these suggestions are for the most part non-verbal, in that students are given considerable support, and are not required to read or write anything too demanding. Obviously then, these types of while-listening task would be better suited to lower-level students. As students gain in confidence and proficiency, while-listening tasks can include more language, for example compiling notes, making predictions, or answering questions with true/false or multiple-choice options.

Intensive listening on the other hand is more concerned with listening for specifics – similar to scan reading. Tasks may involve searching for particular details in a text, identifying words and letters, or completing notes with missing words and numbers.

Post-listening tasks often involve no listening at all, as they frequently require the student to do some sort of follow-up work based on something arising from the listening text itself. This could focus on language items (lexis, structures, functions, sounds) or something based on the topic or theme. Thus post-listening activities could include pronunciation practice or studying a grammatical structure; on the other hand, they could include preparing a speech or a written report using notes taken in a while-listening activity, a role-play based on characters in the text, or further reading or research connected to the theme of the text.

Teacher activity 6.3

Look at some of the listening material in a coursebook you are familiar with. What provision is made for while-listening and post-listening activities? Can you distinguish between extensive and intensive listening tasks, and any listening sub-skills which are required?

Teacher activity 6.4

Using a different coursebook from Teacher activity 6.3, construct pre-, while- and post-listening tasks for some of the listening texts. Try to fit the tasks into your own teaching context.

Reading

We have already established that there are many similarities between the skills of listening and reading, and the pre-, while- and post-tasks outlined above are equally applicable when dealing with a reading text. Furthermore, the principles of purpose and expectation, and bottom-up and top-down approaches, are significant. As with listening skills, the bottom-up and top-down approaches to reading complement, rather than contradict, each other: 'They are both used whenever we read; sometimes one predominates, sometimes the other, but both are needed. And, though normally unconscious processes, both can be adopted as conscious raising strategies by a reader approaching a difficult text' (Nuttall 1996: 16).

In a similar way to listening, bottom-up processing in reading involves the receiver (i.e. the reader) in building up meaning from the smallest identifiable units on the page – the letters become words, the words phrases, the phrases sentences, the sentences paragraphs, and so on. We use this process to double-check something we are unsure about, or if something seems unlikely. We go back to that part of the text and analyse it in detail, but full understanding will only be achieved once we have interpreted the whole text using our previous knowledge, the knowledge already inside our head, in other words using a top-down approach. Good readers move between the two types of processing which 'are in constant interplay. A reader will be involved in ... a continual shift of focus between them' (Hedge 2000: 190).

It is commonly accepted nowadays that readers use different reading sub-skills or strategies when dealing with various texts. In other words, the efficient reader will select a strategy based on the reason(s) for reading. This has already been discussed in earlier chapters.

Teacher activity 6.5

Match the characteristics on the right with the reading sub-skills on the left.

Reading sub-skills	Characteristics
Receptive reading	Rapid search through text to find specific details.
Reflective reading	Reading short story for enjoyment.
Skim reading	Looking carefully at a text for appreciation (e.g. poetry).
Scan reading	Focusing on headings and topic sentences to obtain a global impression.
Intensive reading	Reading, pausing for reflection, and rereading.

Adapted from Pugh (1978) and Lunzer and Gardner (1979), in Hedge (2000: 195)

These real-life purposes in the task above are more and more built into reading activities in ESL and ELT. We need to develop our students' reading skills so that they are comfortable with a range of texts, and so that they can apply various reading strategies, based on particular purposes.

In the **pre-reading** stage, readers are helped to deal with the text through some sort of familiarisation activity, rather than being given a text 'cold', and then answering comprehension questions. Students should be encouraged to think about the purpose of the text, in other words to consider why it was produced, to focus on key lexical items, to express an opinion about the topic or theme of the text, to predict content, to discuss pictures and diagrams associated with the text, and so on. Any of these pre-reading activities will help to raise our students' awareness of the text and familiarise them with it, as well as possibly dispelling any fears they may have about reading it. These types of pre-reading task are very common nowadays in ESL coursebooks.

While-reading tasks allow readers to interact with a text, and motivate them to be active as they read. There are various tasks which can be set to encourage this interaction: ordering ideas in a text, note-taking, putting illustrations in order, finding words with similar (or opposite) meanings, matching headings to paragraphs, replacing gaps in paragraphs with sentences, jigsawing paragraphs or sentences. Once again, the list is endless.

As with listening, **post-reading tasks** will focus on follow-up extension work, usually based on something arising from the text itself, which encourages students to check the things they did while reading. Debates, role-plays and various writing activities are often the preferred options as follow-up activities to a reading text. Of course, language items may be selected by the teacher rather than skill development activities.

Teacher activity 6.6

Look at these sample reading tasks taken from an IGCSE ESL coursebook. Identify the pre-, while- and post-reading activities (original texts not reproduced here).

Exercises 17–27 from Lucantoni, Cox and Glover (2001: 59–64), in jumbled order

1 Match the following words and phrases with one of the four jobs listed. Compare your answers with your partner's.

grass	museum	on court	cups of coffee
200 men and 121 females		auctions	
cover Centre Court in 28 seconds			restaurant

2 Look at the text in more detail and answer the following questions with complete answers.

    a Which two people worked at Wimbledon before their present jobs?

    b Why is bad weather the groundsman's nightmare?

    c What is available for visitors to eat at Wimbledon?

    d What are the main advantages for the umpires of the Millennium Building?

    e What does the curator hope to be doing during her time at Wimbledon?

    f Give three ways in which the museum adds to its collection of memorabilia.

3 The Wimbledon texts include a lot of numbers and dates. What do these numbers and dates refer to?

    Example: 37,000 = The number of people who eat each day at the Club

    a 190,000

    b mid-40s

    c 1977

    d 25 weeks

    e 20-year tenure

    f 1,474

4 What do you think are the most important aspects of a job: a good salary? long holidays? Discuss with your partner and make a list of ideas.

5 Make notes about 'The caterer' text and write your summary. Do not write more than about 70 words.

6 Which definition matches each of the 11 words as used in the texts? Compare your answers with your partner's.

    a appeal, request

    b centre of operations

    c large hole in the ground

    d someone who does not eat meat

    e beginners, students

    f objects made in the past with historical importance

    g grass

    h stand-in workers

    i things connected with a famous person or subject

    j obsessed, worried

    k forecast

7 Skim the texts about people who work at the Wimbledon All England Tennis Club and check your answers to Exercise 20.

8 You are going to read a text introducing some of the people who work at the tennis championships played at Wimbledon. Before you read the text, use your dictionary to check what these jobs are:

caterer   umpire   curator   groundsman

9 You are going to write a short summary of the text about 'The caterer'. First, look at these notes and the summary of the text about 'The umpire':

- Sultan Gangji head umpire
- in charge of 321 umpires from Britain and overseas
- umpires given uniform and training
- aged 16 – 66
- own HQ in Millennium Building
- separate changing-rooms for men and women
- Sultan Gangji also in charge of training and finances

Sultan Gangji is the head umpire at Wimbledon and is in charge of 321 umpires from Britain and overseas, who are aged 16 to 66. After selection, each umpire is given a uniform. The umpires have their own HQ in the Millennium Building, where there are separate changing facilities for men and women. Mr Gangji is also responsible for training the umpires, and for ensuring that all the finances are in order. (72 words)

10 When you finish your education, what job would you like to do? Are there any jobs which you would definitely not like to do? Why?

11 Here are 11 words taken from the four Wimbledon texts. The letters of the words have been mixed up, except for the first letter. Unjumble the letters and write down the words.

Texts	Words
The caterer:	tmpes vgtraeeain
The umpires:	neiovcs hretrauqdaes
The curator:	meoaiilbrma pale actfaters
The groundsman:	piaronad truf certar atcptniiae

We have seen that with both listening and reading, similar approaches can be used in the ESL classroom, and a basic lesson procedure may look something like the one below. This flexible procedure (similar to the 'task-feedback circle' in Scrivener (1994: 150)) is one which I have suggested to teachers on initial pre-service training courses over the years, and which works well:

- **sell it!** – it's unlikely that coursebook material will interest all your students, so you need to generate interest in the topic, and show enthusiasm which will transfer itself to the students.
- **pre-teach** – optional, but invariably there will be some lexical items which are unfamiliar to students, and which can be pre-taught and left on the whiteboard for them to refer to; only pre-teach words which are essential for students to attempt the task successfully, other unknown words can be inferred from the context.
- **pre-task work** – optional, but it helps students if they look through the worksheet, predict, etc., before the task itself is set.
- **gist task** – set the task, give students time to read and digest, and to ask for clarification. Encourage them to predict answer(s) to gist task, and to speculate.
- **listen/read** – do they have to understand every word? No – so tell students! Students complete the task; give them a time limit for reading tasks.
- **feedback** – allow students to check in pairs or groups, and with you; if they have not got gist task correct, explain why answers are wrong – remember that you are not testing them.
- **specific task** – set the task, give students time to read and digest, and to ask for clarification.
- **listen/read** – students complete the task.
- **feedback** – allow students to check in pairs or groups, and with you; consider giving them a copy of the tape script so that they can check answers to task themselves; listen to what your students say in feedback.
- **follow-up** – review the tasks and move on to extension activities.

Speaking

We often make judgements about a person's social, cultural or educational background on the basis of the 'quality' of their spoken language. At the same time, speaking as an L2 skill is often neglected in the classroom, sometimes because teachers themselves may lack confidence in speaking in the target language, or because 'it's not tested in the final examination'. However, the importance of speaking cannot be underestimated as 'our students often need to be able to speak with confidence in order to carry out many of their most basic transactions' (Bygate 1995: vii).

We have already established that there are both similarities and differences between speaking and writing skills. However, one area which we have not mentioned yet is the idea of **reciprocity**. In most speaking situations, the receiver of the message is in close proximity to the speaker. (Of course, there are also situations where this is not the case, such as using the telephone, or a microphone and computer link.) In writing, part of the skill in writing successfully is being able to imagine or predict the other person's point of view, and to make guesses and assumptions about the reader's previous knowledge: 'If the writer gets this wrong, the reader may give up the book or article in disgust ...' (Bygate 1995: 12).

Teacher activity 6.7

Given that in most speaking situations the receiver is in close proximity, what are the implications for the speaker? What does the speaker need to be aware of? Is reciprocity an advantage or a disadvantage? Why?

Obviously, speakers may adapt their utterances based on the physical reaction they observe in the receiver; furthermore, speakers must also be *listeners*, and must pay attention to their listeners' words. To ignore what someone says to you would be regarded as rude or arrogant, or even stupid. Spoken communication is therefore adjusted continually, taking into consideration the physical and vocal signals received. These signals assist the speaker (i.e. the student), but also put pressure on them to acknowledge the other person, to initiate and respond in an appropriate manner, and to understand the importance of taking turns.

As with the skills already discussed, a key factor in the ESL classroom is motivating students, but how can this be done?

Firstly, it can be achieved through making speaking English *relevant* and *purposeful*, by giving them something to do which they are interested in. We need to provide not only topics but also activities which will increase motivation and sustain interest.

Furthermore, as teachers we need to include all aspects of speaking in the classroom, so speaking needs to be integrated with listening – the former is not possible without the latter. Pronunciation practice is also vital, although once again it is too often neglected or relegated.

Also, we cannot expect our students to speak effectively if we have not supplied them with the necessary language, so we have to give them the required language and phrases. A useful starting point for this is 'classroom language', i.e. all the phrases and vocabulary that are useful in everyday classroom situations:

- How do you say XXX in English?
- What's another word for XXX in English?
- Sorry, could you repeat that please?
- What does XXX mean?
- Is there any homework?
- I'm sorry, I don't understand.
- Could you say that more slowly, please?

These phrases can be pinned up around the classroom or next to the board. Very soon students will use them automatically, and will be surprised at how quickly their confidence builds up. The phrases can be added to, with more complex structures being introduced, for example 'What's the difference between "big" and "enormous"?'

Next, provide students with the functional exponents they need in order to carry out pairwork and role-play activities, and demonstrate exactly what they have to do. Then put them in situations where they have to speak in English in order to complete a task. At the same time, we should recognise the importance in monolingual classes in allowing students to use their L1, but only in very (teacher-) controlled circumstances.

Always encourage – do not allow students to become discouraged when they make mistakes. They have to understand that making mistakes is part of the learning process. Be friendly and sensitive to your students.

Make sure your students understand that speakers of English frequently use:

- incomplete sentences;
- very few passive forms;
- not many connectors, such as 'furthermore', 'however', 'on the other hand';
- generalised vocabulary, such as 'nice', 'that stuff', 'thing', 'a lot of';
- repetition;
- pauses and fillers, such as 'erm', 'well', 'yeah', 'got it?', 'I see';

... and that it is all right for them to do the same! However, in a situation such as an examination oral test, students should try to guard against an over-reliance on using too much 'informal' English, and in particular the last three in the list above.

Hedge (2000: 276) states that 'there is a wide range of fluency-based activities available to the teacher', and goes on to discuss three types of activity: free discussion, role play, and 'gap'. In the IGCSE ESL speaking test, students are required to:

> demonstrate competence in a range of speaking activities, e.g. respond to questions on topics within a defined range such as past and present schooling, future plans, current affairs [and] conduct a sustained conversation in a simulation activity [and] show an awareness of audience and an awareness of style and register [and] play a part in a discussion. (CIE 2001: 7)

We need to ensure our students are engaged in activities which encourage them to speak and listen to each other; in other words, activities which get them to communicate. One such activity is the information **gap activity**, in which someone has information which another person does not have: 'the aim ... is to get students to use the language they are learning to interact in realistic and meaningful ways, usually involving exchanges of information' (Scrivener 1994: 62). Thus speaking drills, repetition, reading aloud and so on, while having their uses, are not communicative within Scrivener's definition, nor within my own. Good gap activities are those which do not allow the students to complete the task until they get the information from the other students. Opinion gap activities encourage students to ask and listen because they don't know what other people's opinions are.

Teacher activity 6.8

Look at the speaking activities in a coursebook you are using or one with which you are familiar. What do students have to do? How 'communicative' are the activities?

Free discussion activities involve students in giving their opinions or ideas about a particular topic, agreeing or disagreeing, suggesting alternatives and so on. 'Interpersonal' skills are important here, in other words knowing when to give someone else a turn (i.e. knowing when to listen rather than speak!), and being sensitive to other peoples' opinions. The term 'free' discussion is perhaps somewhat misleading in that it suggests something of a free-for-all situation; however, as Hedge (2000:277) points out, 'discussion usually needs support or structure of some kind'.

So, as with the other skills already discussed, the 'pre-phase' is critical. The teacher may choose to use pictures or text in order to focus the discussion and to encourage students to draw on their previous knowledge, as well as to provide them with key vocabulary and phrases. Apart from anything else, it provides students with that all-important time in which to think and formulate their ideas. It may be that the discussion can take place in stages, with students reporting back periodically once a decision has been made or an agreement has been reached. The teacher will also need to decide if the discussion is to be done in pairs, groups, or whole class; furthermore, will the teacher be involved (at the risk of dominating?), or should they simply be there as an observer and prompter? Some discussion activities can be set up with individual students taking on particular responsibilities, such as chairperson, secretary, or someone who reports back to the whole class.

A further speaking activity, **role play**, is commonly found in English language teaching materials; furthermore, 'I'd do a role play' is often the response made by teachers to the question: 'What would you do next?'! Role-play activities can be an enormous amount of fun for students, and provide excellent opportunities for using language in real-life situations. However, role-play activities which are badly set up by the teacher can be disastrous and a complete waste of time. So, certain 'rules' are necessary:

- Make sure students know what a role-play activity is, and check that they are happy to take on a role.
- As with all activities, check carefully that the context is clear.
- If students have written instructions, make sure they understand them!
- Give enough time for students to read any necessary information and to formulate their ideas. Think about note-taking – are you going to allow it? Can they use dictionaries in this preparation phase?
- Once the activity has started, leave them to it. Monitor, but do not interfere.
- Lastly, make sure you allow time for some sort of feedback or review of the role-play activity.

Teacher activity 6.9

Bearing in mind a particular group of your students, design a speaking activity for them. Remember that the activity should be relevant and purposeful, and ensure that your students have the necessary language. Try to give them a communicative task for completion.

Writing

Because of limited class time, writing may receive insufficient attention from teachers, or be relegated to a homework task. Furthermore, writing has to be read and corrected by the teacher, both of which take up time that could be spent on lesson preparation. Others (teachers and students) may feel that because writing tends to be a 'silent' and reflective activity, it has no place in an active busy classroom. Compared to speaking, writing could be said to fall short in several areas, and several issues deserve attention here (Bowen and Marks 1994: 143–4):

- feedback;
- correction;
- difficulty.

Feedback

In speaking activities, teacher or peer feedback can be more or less instantaneous, providing motivation, encouragement, fun and assistance for students. However, with written work, feedback may be delayed by days or weeks, depending on (a) how quickly the teacher reads and corrects the work; and (b) when the class meets. This delay can cause problems in that students may no longer remember much about the writing task, nor feel that it has any further relevance. Of course, feedback on writing can be done during a lesson, but as the teacher will need to deal with individual students, it may take them away from the class as a whole, and the pace will drop. However, providing students with feedback on their written work is extremely important, and therefore we must all find time to do so, whether such feedback is immediate or delayed.

Correction

Invariably this will come from the teacher, despite the fact that a number of teachers (myself included) advocate self- and peer-correction whenever possible. Returning written work to students with all the corrections made allows no room for self- and peer-correction, which is frequently the procedure with speaking. Students, especially teenagers, tend to be only interested in the mark awarded for their written work, and once they have seen this, the work is often simply discarded without any further interest. Self- and peer-correction, after the teacher has provided feedback (rather than correction of errors), seems nowadays to be the preferred method. Feedback will often take the form of codes, for example 'sp' = spelling error, 'T' = a tense error, and so on. Other teachers may indicate errors by simply underlining them, or by putting a cross in the margin so that students need to reread a particular section or line in order to identify where the mistake is. This type of 'minimal marking' is extremely popular among teachers.

Difficulty

Because of the more formal accuracy required of written English, writing as a skill is often perceived as being more difficult than speaking, in which allowance is made for errors. Students are often able to communicate successfully, despite making mistakes, whereas in writing, mistakes may be regarded as unacceptable, *even if the message is communicated.*

In the IGCSE ESL reading and writing paper, students are required to produce a significant amount of written work, starting with summary writing and note-writing in part 2, and extended writing in part 3. (You may at this stage like to refresh your memory about the writing tasks and have a look at the exercises in the reading and writing paper.) It is probably true to say that 'good' writing cannot be achieved without going through some sort of process, something which is just as true of writing in L1 as in L2.

Teacher activity 6.10

What do you think the 'process' mentioned above is? In other words, what do 'good' writers do when they write?

Good writers think about the 'whole'. This means reading the question carefully and deciding what is required. It involves a consideration of the *purpose* of the activity, and the *audience*, which in turn will indicate to the writer whether a formal or informal register is required. Good writers will also focus initially on general organisation, and may even decide on a suitable number of paragraphs, and whether or not headings and sub-headings would be beneficial (in a report, for example). Brainstorming ideas and making rough notes should be encouraged, as long as teachers also advise students that the point here is to formulate ideas and activate language: just because something has been noted in the planning stage does not mean that it must be used in the writing itself. All of this may be considered as *planning*, and the amount of time spent on this stage of the writing process will vary enormously from one writer to another. There is nothing to suggest that more time spent on planning will result in a better final product, nor is the reverse true – although some planning is essential. Planning can in fact continue during the writing itself, and writers may review their initial ideas as they 'critically evaluate the emerging text and think of new ideas and ways to organise and express them' (Hedge 2000: 306).

What do you think the characteristics of a 'bad' writer might be? Think about some of your students: are they 'good' or 'bad' writers? Why?

During the actual writing phase, writers tend to reflect on what they have already written, and then to move on, having considered how to approach the next 'unit' of writing (which may be a phrase, sentence or paragraph, depending on the student and the task). It is important here for teachers to impress on students that during writing, they should try to focus on the organisation of content, as well as on the accuracy of grammar, as both *content* and *language* are important and are assessed, at least in the IGCSE ESL examination.

Unless writing is being done in an examination situation where time may well be limited, students should be given enough time to write a rough draft before producing a final version. The aim of the rough draft should be for students to get their ideas down on the page, as making sure everything is correct can come later. Having said this, writers who have had little experience of the writing process do tend to find it difficult to 'forget' grammar and spelling, and are constantly distracted by the notion that their writing must be correct, thus forgetting the organisation of its content. Nunan (1991: 87) points out that 'competent writers do not produce final texts at their first attempt', and thus one of our roles as teachers certainly needs to be to discourage students from worrying about correctness until later on in the writing process. However, as already mentioned earlier in this book, another of our roles is to find a balance in our classroom practice; we need to ensure that our students understand the importance of both content *and* language.

Of course, in an examination situation, the time for planning and drafting is extremely limited. I often hear teachers complaining that their students never have enough time to go through the writing process discussed here, and the conclusion many draw is that planning is a waste of time because the examination does not provide for it. However, planning and drafting are skills which need to be developed, and thus a student's ability to plan and draft will improve with practice. With improvement comes speed, and while I would not suggest that examinations provide enough time for preparation before writing, I do believe that with practice and experience of the type of examination questions common in ESL, students should be able to find room for this.

Using a coursebook and examination papers with which you are familiar, analyse the types of writing tasks and make a list (e.g. informal letter, summary, etc.). Then consider what approach you would take in teaching each style.

There are usually no surprises in examination papers, with the types and formats of questions being consistent from one year to the next. This in itself should mean students can be familiar with the types of questions they are likely to have to answer in an examination, and so much of the initial brainstorming of ideas can be reduced to a minimum.

Our work in the classroom must therefore reflect the process which we want our students to move through when engaged in a writing activity: pre-writing (the planning phase), while-writing (reflecting, redrafting, thinking), and post-writing (making changes, editing).

Why not get students to plan together? Getting started is often more difficult than what comes later, so sharing ideas is a good way to overcome this initial hurdle. Alternatively, provide students with points which they can select from (which is what often happens in the IGCSE ESL reading and writing paper). Getting students to make notes is useful, as is arranging ideas in lists, possibly prioritising items. Remember that (as with everything discussed in this book) we are not testing students, but assisting them in the development of their language skills. Also important in the pre-writing stage is for students to focus on their audience and their purpose in writing, as both will obviously affect content. If students have a 'real' audience, the purpose of writing becomes far more interesting and motivating, as well as realistic.

There is no reason why students should not collaborate on their writing. Also, conferencing, where the teacher assists individual students while they write, is becoming increasingly popular. Here a teacher will ask questions, rather than provide answers. For example, the teacher may encourage the student to focus on something with the question 'How should you begin this type of letter?' or 'I think that sentence would be better somewhere else.' Thus students are motivated to reflect and think about their writing, rather than simply rewrite something because the teacher tells them to do so. An interesting while-writing technique is to ask students to write only the first and final paragraphs. This has good results from an organisational point of view as it forces them to think about the 'whole' piece of writing. An extension of this, which involves students collaborating with each other, is for the pieces of writing to be exchanged once the introduction and conclusion have been written! Providing students with a checklist of revisions is another useful way of giving feedback during the writing process, which does not necessarily involve too much of the teacher's attention being focused on individual students.

Obviously it is important for teachers to find time for writing in the classroom. However, writing needs to be supported so that the skill of writing is given an opportunity to develop. Writing tasks need not be complete texts – sentence and paragraph writing are equally as important as 300-word compositions. In fact, it makes sense to restrict writing to sentence and paragraph level until students are confident and competent enough to produce longer texts.

Integrating skills

Having spent much of this chapter discussing language skills in isolation, it seems prudent to conclude by reiterating my thoughts from Chapter 2 about integrated skills. Individual language skills are seldom used in isolation outside the classroom, and should not therefore be learned in isolation inside the classroom. Language skills integrate with each other, and it is vital that this fundamental principle is reflected in whatever we do in the ESL classroom with our students. Classroom tasks which focus on the use of integrated language skills will provide students with a far deeper understanding of how language works, and the tasks themselves should motive and interest students if they are relevant and purposeful.

LOOKING BACK

- How useful is it to have an understanding of top-down and bottom-up approaches to listening and reading?
- What do you now know to be important when designing listening materials?
- Is the amount of time which may be taken up by pre- and post-tasks a concern for you? How could you adapt your lessons to allow for this?
- Which reading sub-skills are the most important for your students? To what extent does it depend on their level?

7 Assessing skills

Assessment is 'the measurement of the ability of a person ... [and] may be by test, interview, questionnaire, observation, etc.' (Richards, Platt and Platt 1996: 23). Whether we like it or not, assessment, in whatever form, is part of the life of a teacher. The purpose of this chapter is not to discuss various tests, nor the rationale behind testing, but to consider the role of the teacher (and student) in assessing the skills in ESL. The term assessment is used here in its broadest sense, and covers not only tests in the traditional manner, but also the monitoring of students' progress during a course of instruction.

How are skills assessed?

There are basically three purposes behind assessment:

- The first is to assess students' current (and sometimes immediate future) status and progress in order to determine what needs to be done in the future, and is commonly referred to as **formative assessment**. This should happen during every lesson, as the teacher listens to students and reads their language efforts. A formative assessment will relate very directly to material covered in the classroom, and students' reactions to it. The main focus is on helping students with the learning process.
- The second purpose is to measure how much students have achieved up to a certain point in time, known as **summative assessment**. This will often take place at the end of a school term or year, and may not be prepared by the class teacher; furthermore, a summative assessment may not relate directly to what has been taught.
- The final purpose is to obtain an external qualification, such as the Cambridge First Certificate in English, IGCSE ESL or TOEFL.

All these types of assessment obviously provide the teacher with varying amounts of feedback. Grades and marks offer limited information to both teacher and student unless they are closely related to written criteria which explain in detail what, for example, 75% or C+ actually mean. A written comment, on the other hand, perhaps complementing a grade or mark, can indicate a student's weaknesses and strengths, and can assist the teacher in highlighting areas for future classroom activities. Moreover, a well-written comment will be far more enlightening to a parent or employer than a simple grade.

We need to ensure that any assessment is fair to everyone, and that it has a positive effect on classroom practice. Despite the problems inherent in testing students, it is possible to use assessment in a beneficial way: there is certainly no doubt that a test encourages the vast majority of students to focus, even if, in some cases, only for a short amount of time! Assessment, however, must be a two-way process in that both teacher and student must benefit from it. As teachers we need to evaluate the assessments we perform in the classroom and ask ourselves if the assessment has worked, and what information was gained from it; could it be improved for the future?

Assessing the skills

In previous chapters I have stressed the importance of teaching *integrated* skills, in other words, avoiding the isolation of individual language skills. It is perhaps ironic therefore that when we come to consider assessment, listening as a skill is, more often than not, tested in isolation. In the 'listening test', students sit, and listen, and have to respond to what they hear by writing something. Rarely are students' listening skills assessed in conjunction with their speaking skills. On the other hand, we have already established that speaking and listening are nearly always integrated, and much assessment of speaking, therefore, also has to consider the student's listening skills. Of course, there are many occasions when an oral (= speaking) assessment is not practicable, whereas an aural (= listening) test can usually be administered fairly easily. Furthermore, when trying to assess more than one skill at the same time, invariably the reliability of the assessment of one skill will suffer for the benefit of the other skill.

Listening and reading

We have already established that listeners and readers need to be proficient in various sub-skills and strategies in order to be efficient: listening or reading for gist, listening or reading for specific details and pieces of information, following instructions or directions, recognising different intonation and stress patterns which may affect meaning, and so on. All of these skills will be vital in the real world, and as such must be developed and assessed in the classroom. Furthermore, in terms of external assessment, it is important that teachers are aware of what will be assessed, and take this into consideration.

Look now at the curriculum content for the IGCSE ESL listening and reading and writing papers (CIE 2001: 7):

Listening

All students must be able to:

+ demonstrate understanding of specific details, information and semi-formal announcements, e.g. news, weather, travel, and in interviews, dialogues and telephone conversations
+ demonstrate general comprehension of the speaker's intentions where appropriate
+ identify the important points or themes of the material they hear, including attitudes
+ draw conclusions from and identify relationships within the material they hear
+ show awareness of major variations in register
+ take notes from material they have heard

Reading

All students must be able to:

+ demonstrate the ability to recognise public notices and signs (including timetables and advertisements)
+ demonstrate the ability to extract relevant specific information from forms, letters, brochures and examples of imaginative writing considered likely to be within the experience of and reflecting the interests of young people from varied cultural backgrounds, including magazines and newspapers likely to be read by young people
+ scan for particular information, organise the relevant information and present it in a logical manner / given format
+ demonstrate the ability to identify the important points or themes within an extended piece of writing
+ draw conclusions from and see relations within an extended text

Teacher activity 7.1

Consider your own classroom practice. What opportunities are there for your students to engage in the activities described in the curriculum content above?

Clearly, the range of sub-skills and strategies is wide, so classroom practice must reflect this. Whenever possible, authentic or near-authentic texts should be used, as in the IGCSE ESL examination itself. The most obvious source for authentic texts is obviously the radio or newspapers and magazines, as well as published teaching materials, and for listening perhaps even recordings made by teachers themselves (although the latter can be very time-consuming and often fraught with problems). However texts are chosen, they will no doubt be of varying length, and include different interaction patterns (monologue, dialogue, interview, etc.) in order to reflect not only the real world, but also the examination assessment objectives quoted above.

Once a listening or reading text has been selected, there are various assessment techniques available to teachers:

- multiple choice;
- short answer;
- note-taking;
- long answer.

Multiple choice

Although this type of question is not normally set in the IGCSE ESL examination, it is commonly used by teachers who write their own tests for both listening and reading. However, good multiple-choice questions are notoriously difficult to write well, and perhaps should be avoided completely, especially by teachers who have had little experience in writing tests. One advantage in using multiple-choice questions is that they are easy to mark; another is that some teachers perceive them as being easy to write! However, 'it is my experience that multiple-choice tests that are produced for use within institutions are often shot through with faults' (Hughes 1994: 61). If multiple-choice questions are to be used as an assessment of students' listening or reading skills, it is important to make sure that the questions have been pre-tested in order to ascertain their reliability. Given that the IGCSE ESL listening and reading examinations do not regularly use these types of question, it may be advisable to employ them sparingly in the classroom.

Short answer

This type of question, which will require only a minimal amount of writing from the student, is particularly useful in that it encourages students to listen or read for specific pieces of information within a text.

The question format could be either (a) a brief question, or (b) part of a sentence requiring completion:

    a What will the weather be like during the day? ....

    b In the afternoon, the weather will be: ....

These questions also encourage students to focus on key words or phrases in the text, rather than on the whole.

Note-taking

Note-taking is a particularly useful real-world listening skill, especially in education, where note-taking in lectures and talks is common. ESL students probably already take notes in their language lessons, and so the use of note-taking as an assessment technique is extremely valuable. Furthermore, it is used extensively in examinations, including the IGCSE ESL examination, where note-*completion* is what really goes on. Students are given a brief written summary (with gaps) of a talk or interview, and are required to listen for the words and numbers which will satisfactorily complete the gaps. Through paraphrasing the language of the text, the questions can be made more demanding, for example:

    Tape script: The island is inhabited by more than twenty-five thousand people.

    Question (gap):   .... people live on the island.

The gapped summary which students have to complete provides them with background language and support for answering the questions. Students need to understand that they do not have to remember everything they hear, but merely show their understanding of the important points, i.e. the points gapped out of the summary.

Although the same technique can be applied to reading, it is not used in the IGCSE ESL examination. However, in some ways it is similar to the sentence-completion-type question described above, in that students are given several phrases and sentences with words gapped out. Students read a text, followed by the gapped summary, and then complete the gaps by referring back to the text. Marking these questions is relatively straightforward, and the amount of writing produced by the student is kept to a minimum.

Long answer

The fourth assessment technique available to teachers is one which requires a longer response from students. One possible drawback here is that the longer the written response required, the more focus there is on the productive skill of writing. Thus, consideration must be given to which skill is actually being assessed: listening/reading or writing (or indeed both?). Examination boards are frequently at pains to point out that listening and reading examinations assess listening, not writing, and that errors in what is written do not count against the student. Of course, if the errors are so serious that they impede communication to the point where the answer is unintelligible, then obviously no marks, or reduced marks, would be awarded.

In the final part of the IGCSE ESL listening examination, students often have to produce longer answers in response to the questions. My experience is that students (and their teachers) are sometimes worried that poor spelling and punctuation, for example, will cause the examiner to mark answers as wrong. However, this is not generally the case. In the classroom, therefore, we must ensure that we provide reward for *understanding* in the assessment of listening, and not penalise students for structural errors which do not affect meaning.

Speaking

While many of us may teach integrated skills, and may prepare students for examinations which contain an assessment of spoken language skills, I wonder how many of us actually assess speaking in the classroom. Students respond to assessment tests, and they provide encouragement to take things seriously. It is important therefore to ensure that speaking is regularly assessed, along with the other skills, in the classroom. However, arranging speaking tests, especially with large numbers of students, can be complex, as well as time-consuming. But the advantages definitely outweigh any disadvantages, and it is worth considering how some form of speaking assessment can be implemented. If your students are preparing for an end-of-course external examination, it makes good sense to work from the curriculum content of that particular examination. The IGCSE ESL syllabus for 2003 (CIE 2001: 7) states:

All students should be able to:
- demonstrate competence in a range of speech activities, e.g. respond to questions on topics within a defined range such as past and present schooling, future plans, current affairs
- demonstrate flexibility in dealing with new, topical ideas
- conduct a sustained conversation in a simulation activity
- show a sense of audience and an awareness of style and register
- play a part in a discussion

Cumulative assessment of speaking skills is probably the least demanding and time-consuming way in which assessment can be done, as keeping a weekly or monthly mark is fairly easy to do. You could use criteria which are examination-specific, for example structure, vocabulary and fluency for the IGCSE ESL speaking examination, or select your own criteria based on, for example, willingness to speak, accuracy, fluency, pronunciation, plus whatever criteria you consider relevant to your particular students. Marks could be 1–5 or A–F for each criterion, or 1–10 in the case of IGCSE. The assessment mark could be based on specific oral activities, such as a role play, as well as general classroom production. If you keep a list of your students' names with you during speaking activities, along with the criteria you are using for assessment, it is not difficult to keep a continuous record. Your record could look something like the one below, using a monthly assessment of structure, vocabulary and fluency. Of course, depending on your requirements, the months could be changed to terms or days or weeks. Similarly, the assessment criteria could be extended.

Criteria		Structure (10)				Vocabulary (10)				Fluency (10)				Total (30)			
Name	Month	Ja	Fe	Ma	Ap	Ja	Fe	Ma	Ap	Ja	Fe	Ma	Ap	Ja	Fe	Ma	Ap
Marios																	
Tandi																	
Katerina																	
Khalid																	

However, given that external examinations of spoken language are not, by definition, based on continuous assessment, you may also wish to conduct short 'interviews' with your students, during which you use the types of questions students are likely to be asked in the examination itself. These are readily available from the boards, and there are plenty of practice tests available from the major publishers. Interviews can be paired or in groups of three, which would reflect the procedure used in UCLES examinations.

Of course, even if your students are not preparing for an external speaking examination, there is no reason whatsoever why you should not use an interview as a form of classroom assessment. In many ways, the 'formality' of an interview encourages students to take speaking more seriously, and, apart from anything else, the assessment itself can be more objective than when it takes place continuously. In an interview, a common set of questions can be given to students, something which will probably not occur during continuous assessment. Furthermore, the teacher's role as assessor is made easier by the fact that they will need to listen to only one or two students at a time, rather than a whole group. The disadvantage of using interviews is that they are very time-consuming, and there is always the problem of what to do with those students who are waiting their turn to be interviewed. In an ideal situation, there would be another teacher available to assist, but this is not always possible.

Whichever approach you decide to use, make sure that your students are not able to see you writing down their marks; on the other hand, in continuous assessment, it is important that students know *when* you are actually assessing them and recording marks.

Making up your own descriptors specific to your own situation is ideal, especially if your students are not preparing for an external examination. Here is a typical example:

Marios	1	2	3	4	5
● Fluency				✓	
● Accuracy					✓
● Content				✓	
Tandi	1	2	3	4	5
● Fluency			✓		
● Accuracy				✓	
● Content				✓	
etc.					

Area	Descriptors
Fluency	Speaks easily, good pronunciation, says a lot (5)
	...
	Needs support, pronunciation difficult to understand, says very little (1)
Accuracy	Few grammatical or language mistakes (5)
	...
	Many mistakes with grammar and language (1)
Content	Good ideas, completes the task effectively (5)
	...
	Few ideas, tasks not completed (1)

You can change the areas for assessment and the descriptors depending on your individual teaching situation, and your needs as a teacher. For example, you may decide that you need to assess your students' abilities to communicate effectively, so 'communication' could be a further assessment area. If you decide that you need to 'weight' each area, you could for example allocate fewer marks to 'accuracy', giving it a maximum of 3 rather than 5.

We have not yet discussed the actual method of grading students, although we have suggested criteria. Obviously, we need a descriptor for each mark available within the specific criterion (e.g. fluency), and different descriptors within each different criterion. Here is the Oral Assessment Criteria Grid for the IGCSE ESL speaking examination:

Oral Assessment Criteria Grid (0510/5 and 0510/6) (CIE 2001)
Give a mark out of 10 for each category (structure, vocabulary and fluency), and then add these marks to give an overall total out of 30.

Mark	Structure [out of 10]	Vocabulary [out of 10]	Fluency [out of 10]
9–10	The candidate demonstrates ability to use a variety of structures accurately and consistently. There may be errors when sophistication is attempted, but the examiner is convinced that the candidate is confidently in control of the structures used.	The candidate shows enough command of vocabulary to respond with some precision. Shades of meaning are achieved and some sophisticated information/ideas are communicated. There will be only the occasional misuse of vocabulary.	The candidate shows sustained ability to maintain a conversation and to contribute at some length. The candidate can respond to change in direction of the conversation and perhaps initiate new topics. Pronunciation and intonation are appropriate, with only the occasional slip.
7–8	There may be mostly simple structures, but some more complex sentences will be attempted successfully. There will be some errors but these will not impede communication.	The candidate has a sufficient range of vocabulary to convey information and ideas but there is lack of precision. Vocabulary is not wide or varied.	The candidate responds relevantly to questions and at a length which makes frequent prompting unnecessary. Stress and intonation patterns are generally accurate. Little effort is required by the listener.

Mark	Structure [out of 10]	Vocabulary [out of 10]	Fluency [out of 10]
5–6	The candidate will be uneasy and error-prone when venturing beyond simple structures. However, simple accuracy will often be achieved and communication will be maintained.	Vocabulary conveys simple ideas and information clearly but lacks precision. There is some searching for words and hesitation when going beyond simplicity.	The candidate makes a real attempt to respond to questions. S/he may need frequent prompting and will tend to offer one sentence at a time, but keeps conversation going. Some noticeable inaccuracy of stress and intonation, but unlikely to impede communication.
3–4	Responses will usually be single words or very simple sentences – with errors. Error will tend to blur but not obscure communication.	Vocabulary will sometimes be inadequate to convey even simple ideas and there will be frequent pauses.	Responses tend to be brief and widely spaced. The candidate has to be encouraged to go beyond the single word response. Stress and intonation inaccuracy causes some communication difficulty, but candidate can usually be understood by a sympathetic listener.
1–2	Single word responses will be the norm and attempts at structured sentences will rarely achieve communication. However, some attempt at a response will be made at points during the interview.	Enough English words are known to convey occasional snippets of information, but conversation will be very limited and confused.	Responses are so brief and imprecise that little is communicated. Use of single words is the norm, and there will be long gaps. Stress and intonation patterns cause difficulty for even the most sympathetic listener. Repetition is necessary to achieve communication.
0	Completely limited/no attempt at a response.	Completely limited/no attempt at a response.	No response/inaccuracy of stress and intonation prevents communication even after several repetitions.

Making up your own descriptors specific to your own situation is ideal, especially if your students are not preparing for an external examination.

Writing

At advanced ESL levels, student writing tends to be of the more extensive type, i.e. letters, reports, reviews, summaries and so on, rather than the more controlled writing (transformations, error-recognition, changing words, writing short notes and paragraphs, etc.) suitable for lower levels. Assessment therefore will be more holistic, and in many respects more complex with advanced levels where we would expect our students to be producing original, imaginative pieces of writing.

As mentioned in previous chapters, it is important that students have a purpose and an audience for their writing, and this should be reflected in whatever scheme of assessment is used for written work. As with the assessment of speaking, we should assess written work against certain criteria, within which there are descriptors. Teachers often complain that they have no idea how to assess their students' writing, but the most efficient way is to work with criteria and descriptors. Below is an example taken from Lucantoni (2001: 16–17) of the descriptors used to assess extended writing in the IGCSE ESL reading and writing examination. The philosophy is that candidates should be given credit for their efforts, and thus a positive approach is taken when marking – reward is given for achievements, rather than taking away marks for mistakes.

Grade A (12/12, 15–16/16)[1]
The language is accurate; occasional errors are either slips or arise from attempts to use ambitious structures or vocabulary that may be imperfectly understood. Vocabulary is wide enough to convey intended shades of meaning with some precision. Sentences show some variation of length and type. Punctuation is accurate and generally helpful. Spelling is nearly always accurate. Paragraphs show some evidence of planning, have unity and are usually appropriately linked. The response is relevant, and the interest of the reader is aroused and sustained throughout most of the composition.

Grade B (10–11/12, 13–14/16)
Vocabulary and structures are mainly correct when they are simple; mistakes may occur when more sophistication is attempted. Sentences may show some variety of structure and length, although there may be a tendency to repeat sentence types and shapes. Spelling of simple vocabulary is accurate, although errors may

[1]Note that the marks shown refer to the syllabus at the time of publication.

occur when more difficult tasks are attempted, e.g. the punctuation of direct speech. Sentence separation is correct. The composition is written in paragraphs which may show unity, although some links may be absent or inappropriate. The composition is relevant and will arouse some interest in the reader.

Grade C (7–9/12, 10–12/16)
The meaning is clear. There will be patches of accurate language, particularly when simple vocabulary and structures are used. Vocabulary is usually adequate to convey intended meaning, although it may be insufficiently developed to achieve precision. Idiom may be uncertain at times. Punctuation will be used, but may not enhance/clarify meaning. Some sentence separation errors may occur occasionally. Simple words will be spelt accurately, but more complex vocabulary may show spelling weaknesses. Paragraphs will be used but may lack unity or coherence. A genuine attempt has been made to address the topic, but there may be digressions or failures of logic.

Grade D (5–6/12, 7–9/16)
Meaning is never in doubt, but the errors are sufficiently frequent and serious to hamper precision, and may slow down speed of reading. Some simple structures will be accurate, but the script is unlikely to sustain accuracy for long. Vocabulary may be limited, either too simple to convey precise meaning or more ambitious but imperfectly understood. Some idiomatic errors are likely. Simple punctuation will usually be accurate, but there may be frequent sentence separation errors. Paragraphs may lack unity or be used haphazardly. The subject matter will show some relevance.

Grade E (3–4/12, 5–6/16)
There will be many serious errors of various kinds throughout the script, but they will be of the single-word type, i.e. they could be corrected without re-writing the sentence. Communication is established, although the weight of error may cause blurring from time to time. Sentences will probably be simple and repetitive in structure. Vocabulary will convey meaning, but is likely to be simple and imprecise. Errors in idiomatic usage will be a significant feature. Spelling may be inconsistent. Paragraphing may be haphazard or non-existent. There may be evidence of relevant subject matter, but the weight of linguistic error will tend to obscure or neutralise its effect.

<u>Grade F (2/12, 3–4/16)</u>
Sense will usually be decipherable but some of the errors will be multiple, i.e. requiring the reader to reread and re-organise before meaning becomes clear. There are unlikely to be more than a few accurate sentences, however simple, in the whole composition. The content is likely to be comprehensible, but may be partly hidden by the density of the linguistic error.

<u>Grade G (1/12, 1–2/16)</u>
Scripts are entirely, or almost entirely impossible to recognise as pieces of English writing. Whole sections will make no sense at all. Where occasional patches of relative clarity are evident some marks will be given. The mark of 0 is reserved for scripts that make no sense at all from beginning to end.

This type of assessment also allows for weighting of particular criteria. In other words, if you feel that vocabulary needs to be emphasised because your students tend to be repetitive, for example, you could double the number of marks available under 'vocabulary range'. On the other hand, if you wanted to impress on your students that you are keen for them to focus on content, you could reduce the number of marks available for grammar and spelling. The assessment criteria can therefore work as excellent motivators for your students. The great advantage in using this method is that the teacher is able to adjust the scheme depending on particular circumstances.

I am aware of teachers who use an assessment method which involves counting errors – a half mark is deducted for every mark the teacher can find in the written work; however, this method, while very easy to administer(!), takes no account of the seriousness of particular errors and, more importantly, it discounts content. If the only criterion for assessment is based on finding errors, and no credit is given for communication, there will be little motivation for students to want to write. Certainly it is an assessment method which is not to be recommended.

A second method is based on the reader's *impression* of what the student has written. This is a suitable method where large numbers of scripts need to be marked, in a school at the end of the term or year, for example. Assessors glance through the scripts, *without actually reading them in detail,* and give a mark based on their overall impression of the writing. The scripts are then handed over to a second marker, and even a third marker where large numbers are involved. The marks of each marker are then added together, and either an average or a total mark is awarded. In cases of clear disagreement, the script in question would be read in detail and discussed in order to arrive at a consensus. Clearly in a classroom situation this impression assessment method would not be satisfactory; apart from anything else, it does not allow for feedback to students indicating their strengths and weaknesses.

Feedback should of course encourage students. Obviously, the more productive feedback the students receive, the more likely they are to want to write more. The method I use is to list 2–3 strengths under a ✓, and 2–3 'things to work on' under a ?. Furthermore, I always add a final comment which summarises what the student has achieved. For example:

✓	?
wide range of appropriate vocab	check subject / verb agreements
excellent conclusion	paragraphing weak
logical progression of ideas	3rd paragraph is confusing

Maria – Overall this is a good effort. You have answered the question. You need to think more about how to break up your ideas into paragraphs, and check for errors with subject and verb. I enjoyed reading your report. Well done.

Teacher activity 7.2

Consider the feedback method described above. Is it a method that you would implement in your teaching situation, if you do not already use it? If not, why not?

A very productive and student-centred approach to assessing writing in the ESL classroom is to use formative assessment. Here, the evaluation of a piece of writing leads to some form of teaching and learning in the classroom. In other words, the teacher responds to any problems noted in the students' written work, in a similar way to when a teacher responds to classroom oral errors. The teacher is thus responding to students' needs. Taken further, formative assessment can lead to changes in the overall curriculum for future students at a similar level.

A variation of assessment is for teachers to encourage their students to assess each other's written work, using guidelines provided by the teacher. In this way, students have an idea of what to look for, and are encouraged to avoid simply looking for errors of structure and spelling.

Usually, students enjoy reading the work of their friends and colleagues and, apart from anything else, they are given an opportunity to do some reading in English! Obviously teachers need to monitor and note any problems in their students' writing for feedback later.

There may be occasions during a course when the teacher decides that written work should not be assessed at all, nor even read by the teacher. One of my colleagues introduced me to the idea of students having a pen-friend within the school. Here is how to set up this writing activity:

- You need two or three classes of similar level with more or less equal numbers in each class.
- Each student decides on a suitable nickname.
- Students are then provided with an exercise book which is going to be their journal or diary.
- Each student writes their first journal entry, which should be some sort of introduction to their new 'unknown' pen-friend, and signs with their new nickname.
- The teacher collects all the journals from one class, and distributes them to a second class.
- The students in the second class reply to the journal entries from the first class, and so on.

It is important that the students understand that their teachers will never read their journals, and that their writing will never be corrected. They should also attempt to remain anonymous for as long as possible! However, they should understand that what they are doing is an authentic writing activity, and as such will help them to develop their writing skills.

Assessing writing is never an easy task. However, it can be a less demanding activity for us if we provide ourselves with descriptors, and attempt to introduce some variety into the way we assess.

 LOOKING BACK

- ◆ How important is assessment in your situation?
- ◆ Having read this chapter, how confident do you feel in the assessment of your students in the various skills?
- ◆ How much time do you dedicate to marking students' written work? Is this a problem? If so, how could you address it?
- ◆ Would it be feasible in your situation to ask students to write something which will not be assessed? How comfortable would you feel with this?

8 Conclusion

I pointed out in the introductory chapter that I hoped this book would prove useful to ESL teachers worldwide who are involved in teaching English at IGCSE and similar levels. I have attempted to cover those areas which I feel are of importance to teachers, and in doing so have based what I have written here on my own past and current experiences of teaching ESL at advanced levels, with a strong focus on developing language skills through a student-centred approach. I hope that people who read this book will not see my words as being dogmatic about teaching, but rather as an attempt to promote some debate about the issues of teaching and developing the language skills in ESL. Without debate, there is unlikely to be reflection by teachers on their current practices; without reflection, there is unlikely to be change.

I also hope that this book has been accessible to readers. Far too often I hear the complaint that EFL/ESL journals and texts are too difficult to read and full of jargon which distracts the reader from understanding the meaning of the words. While in any profession there are bound to be terms which are subject-specific, I would like to think that any teachers who have chosen to dip into this book will not have been bemused by technical terminology.

For those teachers who have not yet had the opportunity to attempt any of the approaches and techniques suggested, I hope that you will be able to do so soon. Of course, there may be any number of reasons for not doing so, but I would like to think that perhaps some of the things I have suggested would apply to your particular teaching situations. As I said in the introduction, there is no right or wrong way to teach, only more or less effective ways to teach. However, one would hope that we are all trying to achieve the same goals.

Change, or doing something differently in the classroom, is always difficult. It is far easier to continue doing things in the same tried and tested way, even though we may realise that there is another way of doing something. My advice to busy teachers is to have a go and see what happens, because you may get a pleasant surprise. If your students are reluctant to change their ways, ensure that you point out the benefits of approaching something from a different angle. Even if you (and your students) make the decision not to change, at least you will have tried something new, and you will have reflected on your teaching and your students' situations for learning.

Appendix A: References and resources

References cited in the text

Bowen, T. and Marks, J. 1994. *Inside teaching*. Heinemann.

Brown, G. and Yule, G. 1983. *Teaching the spoken language*. Cambridge University Press.

Bygate, M. 1995. *Speaking*. Oxford University Press.

CIE 2001. *IGCSE English as a Second Language – syllabus for examination in 2003*. Cambridge International Examinations.

Crystal, D. 1999. *The Cambridge encyclopedia of the English language*. Cambridge University Press.

Finocchiaro, M. and Brumfit, C. 1983. *The functional–notional approach: from theory to practice*. Oxford University Press.

Harmer, J. 2000. *The practice of English language teaching*. Longman.

Hedge, T. 2000. *Teaching and learning in the language classroom*. Oxford University Press.

Hughes, A. 1994. *Testing for language teachers*. Cambridge University Press.

Hymes, D. H. 1972. 'On communicative competence'. In J. B. Pride and J. Holmes (eds.), *Sociolinguistics*. Penguin.

Johnson, R. K. 1981. 'On syllabus and being communicative'. *The English Bulletin (Hong Kong)*, 7/4: 52–60.

Lucantoni, P. 2001. *IGCSE English as a Second Language: teacher's book*. Cambridge University Press.

Lucantoni, P., Cox, M. and Glover, R. 2001. *IGCSE English as a Second Language*. Cambridge University Press.

Lunzer, E. and Gardner, K. 1979. *The effective use of reading*. Heinemann.

McDonough, J. and Shaw, C. 2000. *Materials and methods in ELT – a teacher's guide*. Blackwell.

Nunan, D. 1991. *Language teaching methodology – a handbook for teachers*. Prentice Hall International.

Nuttall, C. 1996. *Teaching reading skills in a foreign language*. Heinemann.

Pugh, A. K. 1978. *Silent reading*. Heinemann.

Richards, J. C. and Rodgers, T. S. 2000. *Approaches and methods in language teaching*. Cambridge University Press.

Scrivener, J. 1994. *Learning teaching*. Heinemann.

Skilbeck, M. 1984. 'A framework for the implementation of task-based instruction'. *Applied Linguistics*, 17/1: 38–62.

UCLES 1999. *CAE Certificate in Advanced English handbook*. University of Cambridge Local Examinations Syndicate.

UCLES 1997. *IGCSE standards in English as a Second Language*. University of Cambridge Local Examinations Syndicate.

White, R. V. 1981. 'Reading'. In Johnson and Morrow (eds.), *Communication in the classroom*. Longman.

Willis, J. 1991. *A framework for task-based learning*. Longman.

Recommended resources
Books

Alderson, L. and Aspinall, P. 1997. *International English – English for the IGCSE ESL examination*. Macmillan.

Barr, I. and Walton, C. 1998. *GCSE questions and answers English for 1999 exams*. Letts.

Barry, M. 1998. *Success international – English skills for IGCSE*. Georgian Press.

Carter, R. and Nunan, D. (eds.). 2001. *The Cambridge Guide to teaching English to speakers of other languages*. Cambridge University Press.

Cox, M. and G. 1990. *International GCSE English*. Phoenix ELT.

Davies, S., Elliot, K. and Hopwood, R. 1997. *GCSE English – a complete course*. Heinemann.

Dudeney, G. 2000. *The Internet and the language classroom*. Cambridge University Press.

du Vivier, M., Hopkis, A. and Potter, J. 1994. *Look Ahead teacher development worksheets*. Longman.

Gower, R., Phillips, D. and Walters, S. 1995. *Teaching practice handbook*. Heinemann.

James, P. 2001. *Teachers in action*. Cambridge University Press.

Richards, J., Platt, J. and Platt, H. 1996. *Dictionary of language teaching and applied linguistics*. Longman.

Seely, J. 1998. *Understanding – a GCSE Course*. Oxford University Press.

Seely, J. et al. 1997. *Get it right!* Heinemann.

Skehan, D. 1998. *A cognitive approach to language learning*. Oxford University Press.

Willis, J. and Willis, D. (eds.). 1996. *Challenge and change in language teaching*. Heinemann.

Journals

English Teaching Professional (ETp), 12 Kent Road, Chiswick, London, W4 5EZ, UK. www.etprofessional.com

English Language Teaching Journal (ELTJ) (published by Oxford University Press). www.eltj.oupjournals.org

EL Gazette, 5th Floor, Dike House, 1 Malet Street, Bloomsbury, London, WC1E 7JN, UK. www.elgazette.com

Modern English Teacher (published by Pearson Education). www.onlinemet.com

The Guardian Weekly, 75 Farringdon Road, London, EC1M 3HQ, UK. www.guardianweekly.com

Web-based resources

www.bbc.co.uk/worldservice/learningenglish
www.englishclub.com
www.eteach.com
www.link2english.com
www.onestopenglish.com
www.teach-nology.com/web_tools/youngwordsearch
www.theeducatorsnetwork.com/utt/vocabuilder.htm

Appendix B: Useful addresses

Publishers

Cambridge University Press, The Edinburgh Building, Shaftesbury Road, Cambridge CB2 2RU, UK. www.cambridge.org

DELTA Publishing, 39 Alexandra Road, Addlestone, KT15 2PQ, UK. www.deltapublishing.co.uk

Macmillan Education, Between Towns Road, Oxford, OX4 3PP, UK. www.macmillaneducation.com

Mary Glasgow Magazines, Commonwealth House, 1–19 New Oxford Street, London, WC1A 1NU, UK. www.link2english.com

Oxford University Press, Great Clarendon Street, Oxford, OX2 6DP, UK. www.oup.com

Pearson Education (Longman), Edinburgh Gate, Harlow, CM20 2JE, UK. www.pearsoned-ema.com

Examination boards and other organisations

British Association of Lecturers in English for Academic Purposes (BALEAP). www.baleap.org.uk

The British Council, 10 Spring Gardens, London, SW1A 2BN, UK. www.trs.britishcouncil.org

Educational Testing Service, Rosedale Road, Princeton, NJ 08541 USA. www.toefl.org

International Association of Teachers of English as a Foreign Language (IATEFL), 3 Kingsdown Chambers, Whitstable, CT5 2FL, UK. www.iatefl.org

LCCI Examinations Board. www.lccieb.com

Pitman Qualifications, 1 Giltspur Street, London, EC1A 9DD, UK. www.pitmanqualifications.com

Trinity College London, 89 Albert Embankment, London, SE1 7TP, UK. www.trinitycollege.co.uk

University of Cambridge Local Examinations Syndicate Cambridge International Examinations, 1 Hills Road, Cambridge, CB1 2EU, UK. www.cie.org.uk

University of Cambridge Local Examinations Syndicate, English as a Foreign Language, 1 Hills Road, Cambridge, CB1 2EU, UK. www.cambridge-efl.org.uk

VSO, 317 Putney Bridge Road, London, SW15 2PN, UK. www.vso.org.uk

Appendix C: Glossary

activity	Used to help students achieve the lesson aims. Thus a role-play activity may be used by a teacher to help achieve the aim of improving students' fluency
assessment	The collection of information concerning a student's achievements and proficiency
bottom-up processing	Understanding text by putting together information from phonological, lexical, grammatical and discoursal parts
CALL	Computer assisted language learning
CLT	Communicative language teaching, where the teaching and learning goal is competence in language communication
curriculum	The aims, methods, techniques and evaluation processes of a subject
EFL	English as a foreign language – the term used to describe the role of English in countries where English is not the L1, but is taught as a subject in schools. Note that in the US the term EFL is not in common use; the term ESL is used instead
ESL	English as a second language – the term used to describe the role of English in countries where English is not the L1, but is used widely in education, business and commerce
extensive reading	Reading in some quantity, and in order to broaden effective and efficient reading habits, and to increase a student's range of vocabulary and structure
follow-up activities	Activities used by a teacher to consolidate or extend students' use of language

formative assessment	An assessment of students in order to assist them with the learning process; in other words, an assessment of current status and progress. Usually relates very closely to what has been taught in the classroom
goals	Long-term aims, described in general terms
integrating skills	The use of more than one language skill at the same time, rather than the use of skills in isolation
intensive reading	Usually requires a detailed understanding of a text
key words	Terms/words that can help students identify those words which may lead them to answers in a text
language proficiency	The ability of a student to use L2 for communication
language skills	A student's abilities in using a language – reading and listening (receptive) and speaking and writing (productive)
language sub-skills	Divisions of skills – for example, in reading, we apply different reading strategies depending on our reading purpose and the type of text
student-centred approach	A teaching approach which focuses on and considers students' needs and expectations
lesson aims	Things that students should be able to do, or the language that they should be able to use, by the end of the lesson, that they could not do or use at the start
needs analysis	A process in order to determine and prioritise the needs for which a student requires a language; the examination of a student to determine what they need to be able to do in L2
productive skills	Speaking and writing active skills
receptive skills	Reading and listening – sometimes called passive skills

register	The variations in a person's speech or writing depending on their purpose and audience – sometimes referred to as style or stylistic variety
reliability	The extent to which a test measures consistently
scanning	Reading sub-skill, used to find specific facts or details
skimming	Reading sub-skill, used to obtain an overall idea of text content
style	See register
summative assessment	An assessment of students, usually at the end of the school term or year, which may not relate directly to what has been taught in the classroom
task-based approach	Using tasks rather than vocabulary and grammar as the basis for a syllabus, which provide a real purpose in using language
top-down processing	Understanding text by making an appraisal of what ought to be there, using background knowledge
validity	The extent to which a test measures what it claims to measure

Index

Other titles in the Professional Development for Teachers series

Teaching and Assessing Skills in Accounting	ISBN 978-0-521-54367-5
Teaching and Assessing Skills in Bussiness Studies	ISBN 978-0-521-54366-8
Teaching and Assessing Skills in Computer Studies	ISBN 978-0-521-75360-9
Teaching and Assessing Skills in Economics	ISBN 978-0-521-54825-0
Teaching and Assessing Skills in First Language English	ISBN 978-0-521-75355-5
Teaching and Assessing Skills in Foreign Languages	ISBN 978-0-521-60103-0
Teaching and Assessing Skills in Geography	ISBN 978-0-521-75357-9
Teaching and Assessing Skills in Mathematics	ISBN 978-0-521-75361-6
Teaching and Assessing Practical Skills in Science	ISBN 978-0-521-75359-3